Happily Ever After...?

An Essential Guide
To Successful Relationships

D0279902

Splendid
PUBLICATIONS

Happily Ever After...?

An Essential Guide
To Successful Relationships

Splendid

PUBLICATIONS

**Janet Clegg and
Hilary Browne Wilkinson**

Happily Ever After...?
An Essential Guide To Successful Relationships
Janet Clegg and Hilary Browne Wilkinson

Splendid Publications Ltd
Unit 7
Twin Bridges Business Park
South Croydon
Surrey CR2 6PL

www.splendidpublications.co.uk

British Library Cataloguing in Publication Data is available from The British Library

ISBN: 9781909109681

Designed by Chris Fulcher at Swerve Creative Design & Marketing Ltd.
www.swerve-creative.co.uk

Printed and bound by CPI Group (UK) Ltd., Croydon, CR0 4YY

Commissioned by Shoba Vazirani
Edited by Ros Jesson

Contents

Introduction

Janet Clegg and **Hilary Browne Wilkinson** practised as divorce lawyers in London and Hong Kong.

In our time as lawyers we saw into the inner workings of several hundred failed relationships of couples who came from many and varied backgrounds and cultures. We empathised with the untold misery and sense of loss that most individuals felt on the breakdown of a long-term relationship but we were struck by how many couples we saw who had embarked on marriage or long-term cohabitation with less thought as to whether their potential partner was a good fit for a long and happy life together than they would give to choosing a new car or phone contract.

We were even more surprised how time and time again the people we saw were prepared to jump immediately into a new relationship even if their previous marriage or partnership had come to a sticky and acrimonious end. It would seem that, contrary to previous experience, the flame of hope continued to burn brightly that things would be better with another person and that somewhere 'out there' the ideal soulmate was waiting to wipe out all past horrendous emotional experiences.

Oscar Wilde was no stranger to the pitfalls of choosing the

wrong partner. And maybe he was a little jaundiced when he said, 'Marriage is the triumph of imagination over intelligence. Second marriage is the triumph of hope over experience,' as recent research shows that second marriages have a marginally better chance of survival than first marriages. Still, nearly 42% of marriages seemed doomed to failure and in the UK more than 235,000 couples divorced in 2011. It is thought about one in eight separated or divorced fathers in the UK have no contact with their children.

These statistics show only the ending of marriages and not long-term partnerships and they only show the bold maths of a divorce and not the backstory of the substantial emotional and financial turmoil suffered by the individuals, the many children caught up in a relationship break-up and indeed our society as a whole. Research carried out by the Marriage Foundation in 2015 estimates that family breakdown costs the UK £47 billion a year in increased tax credits, benefits and other knock-on effects on children.

In the West, so many of us subscribe to the idea that somewhere out there, if only we look hard enough, we will find our soulmate. Blame the Ancient Greeks for that one. Plato wrote about the Ancient Greek myth that all humans were originally created with four arms, four legs and a head with two faces. Zeus, the King of the Gods, decided to split the being into two separate parts, scattering the fragments across the world, which condemns us humans to forever search for our complementary half. And, of course, some people do find that elusive soulmate, the perfect partner and the love of their lives.

The ninety-five-year-old mother of a good friend was married for over sixty-five years and on her husband's death, when he was ninety-three, said, 'I have been lucky. I was born into a loving family and I had a loving marriage all my life.'

But is it luck? Can you raise the odds on a long and happy partnership? Surely in the twenty-first century finding our soulmate should be so much simpler. In the last forty years we have had the loosening of attitudes to sex, cohabitation, divorce and the acceptance of same-sex relationships, having children without marriage and meeting a partner through the myriad of opportunities that the internet gives us. Economically women are less dependent on men and, indeed, in a growing number of relationships women are the breadwinners and men are choosing to stay at home to raise children. Ostensibly, we now have the tools and the freedom to seek out the perfect mate, wherever in the world they may be. If we are a Jane Austen-loving Goth living in the Falklands there is no problem because surely there will be someone out there for us (albeit living in Greenland!).

But as a society it would seem we are far from being happier than previous generations. Mental health problems in the young are soaring and in 2012 more than 50 million prescriptions for antidepressants were issued. It is a bold statement of fact that difficulties within relationships have the capacity to make us extremely unhappy.

And if relationships can make so many of us so very unhappy, what is the point of them? Are relationships always just for mutual love and support? Are relationships there purely to satisfy our sexual needs or our wish for financial security or status or is it simply that we are so afraid of being alone that we cling to any relationship, no matter how damaging?

At their very best relationships can sustain us on our path through life and it is certain that in committing to a partnership, whether or not it lasts, all areas of our lives will be forever affected (and, inevitably, if we have children theirs too).

There are hundreds of books out there that promise to find you the love of your life, tell you how to keep the love of your life or help you find out why the love of your life is from Uranus (cheap pun intended) so how can two former divorce lawyers add anything new? We feel that as a result of our experiences through our professional and personal lives we can pass on valuable pointers to help couples, already in a committed relationship, limit the possibility of the failure of a long-term relationship. Too often we saw the wrong end of relationships – the failed, messy and sometimes downright dangerous end – and in our opinion most failed relationships came unstuck because of the failure of one or more of the following four basic principles:

1. Realism
2. Integrity
3. Self-awareness
4. Knowledge: practical and legal

A lack of any of the above four principles can put a strain on any relationship, be it a work, friendship or an intimate one. Being wildly unrealistic or dishonest (with others or ourselves) will only lead to bitter disappointment when the reality of the situation becomes clear. A lack of self-awareness can lead to relationship failure again and again and a lack of knowledge about financial and more practical matters will ensure that you will constantly make ill-informed decisions, particularly about money.

Even the best relationships have their own 'Achilles heel'; that soft, vulnerable part of the relationship that causes more arguments and problems than anything else. The following chapters are intended to get you to take a long, hard look at yourself as well as your partner. We want you to think about what you hope to get from your emotional partnerships. We want you to be able to flag up potential problems before they become insurmountable so that you are able to avoid possible future emotional turmoil. And we want you to be able to make well-informed decisions about financial and other practical matters.

Our emotional lives can lead us on a journey that can be exhilarating, terrifying, satisfying and wonderful, with the chance that if we have been given bad emotional equipment for the trip we can lose control and end up damaged. We hope that this book can give you the tools to limit that potential damage.

So, this is not the book that will tell you how to track down the ideal partner, it's not the book if you like to play mind games with your partner or believe *Fifty Shades of Grey* is the perfect template for a successful relationship. This is the book that will try to give you a good chance of making a committed relationship endure the ups and downs of life. It can be used by anyone at any stage in a relationship, whether you are setting off on a new relationship with long-term potential or if you have been together for years and wish to mend and repair a struggling relationship.

We have drawn on sources from our own experiences through our past work and personally, literature, old and new, and from contemporary newspaper and magazine articles. Most chapters contain a self-reflective element to them. There are no right or wrong answers to the questions we ask as they are intended to either provoke discussion with your partner or to get you to consider honestly your own part in your relationship. The more aware you are of your hopes about the relationship the better you are able to participate positively in that relationship and the more knowledge you have about the practical and legal aspects the better you are able to make informed decisions at every stage of that relationship.

We hope that our experiences at the 'wrong end' of relationships (the total failure and breakdown of the relationship) can help you to keep your own partnership on track so that you are able to experience the happiness we all so richly crave and deserve.

***

Whilst every care has been taken to check the accuracy of any information given in our book it is not intended to be a substitute for professional legal or financial or emotional advice or guidance. No case studies mentioned within this book refer to any specific individual, couple or family who we might have encountered within our professional careers and are intended for illustrative purposes only.

Janet Clegg and Hilary Browne Wilkinson

Chapter One
Love

'The course of true love never did run smooth.'
—**William Shakespeare**

Love and happiness

Most of us have the fundamental assumption that love will bring happiness. Usually we seek happiness in a partnership but here is the first reality warning! Love is not necessarily synonymous with happiness. Love is an emotion that exists between two or more people. Happiness is our own state of mind.

Alexandra Fuller, in her book, *Leaving Before The Rains Come*, wisely says, *'It's not anyone's job to make another person happy, but the truth is, people can either be very happy or very unhappy together. Happiness or unhappiness isn't a measure of their love. You can have an intense connection to someone without being a good lifelong mate for him. Love is complicated and difficult that way.'*

In our experience the pursuit of happiness by abandoning a partner to take up with another never seemed to lead to long-term contentment. No matter how single-minded we are, it's hard to leave behind a trail of bitter ex-partners and devastated children without there being some sort of consequence rained down upon our heads at a later date.

But as we all know, falling in love can be sublimely wonderful. How many times in the course of our practice did we hear the words, 'I feel that until now I have been sleep-walking through my life. Being in love has made everything so real'? In fact, being in love is the exact opposite; everything is very unreal. The danger is that when we fall in love we will look to our partner to become everything to us, to complete us and fulfil our hopes that, at last, we have found our long-lost soulmate and that 'happy ever after' is surely guaranteed.

The harsh and sad truth is that it is virtually impossible for another human being to be our perfect match, although we may be more compatible with some than others.

Falling in love and entering into a committed relationship is always a blind act of faith, a leap into the terrifying abyss of the unknown, no matter how propitious the circumstances, how well suited you seem in your family connections, common interests or shared religious, political, cultural or educational backgrounds.

Love is such a small word but it encompasses such a huge range of emotions. It has, of course, inspired poets, artists and writers throughout the centuries but it has also been used to justify murder itself. Several countries in the world still treat 'crimes of passion' with a greater tolerance than might be expected in the twenty-first century.

***

Mythical love

The Ancient Greeks, whose myths still inform psychotherapeutic writings, worshipped Aphrodite, the Goddess of Love, and in that mythology Aphrodite's great passion for gorgeous Adonis eventually led to the Trojan War. Love for the Ancient Greeks was full of potential for danger, madness or even death. The Gods made fools of ordinary mortals and their desire for love. Oedipus killed his father then fell in love and married his mother and Medea fell madly in love with Jason during his quest for the Golden Fleece but ended up killing their children after he jilted her for another woman. Even poor old Narcissus faded away after falling in love with himself, despite the attempts of admirers to entice him into a relationship with them.

The most random and cursory trawl of newspapers and magazines in the twenty-first century shows that themes described in the Ancient Greek myths are still being played out in modern-day family relationships. A drug addict kills his father, admittedly not for the love of his mother but for an inheritance to fund his habit. A grief-stricken mother kills her three children after being abandoned by her partner for another, and time and time again stepfathers kill the child of their partner. Perhaps this can be explained by primitive biology: a man is programmed to eradicate the progeny of another man. Or is it that a child unrelated by blood who has a greater claim on the love and attention of the partner is a threat that cannot be ignored?

***

The chemistry of love

Psychological research has shown that falling in love releases various hormones in both female and male brains that alter the chemical make-up of the brain. That would explain why when we feel we are in love we experience elevated happiness, butterflies in the stomach and, much, much more dangerously, the tendency to exaggerate the virtues or overlook the glaring flaws of our partners.

'But when you're in love nothing is so abstract or horrible that it can't be thought of as cute' —David Sedaris.

It seems that this heightened state of emotion can last up to thirty months or so, after which the slow realisation of the reality of our relationship begins to dawn upon us. That is why the quirky traits and charming eccentricities of our beloved that were all so adorable and amusing at the beginning of the relationship can transform into appalling and irritating habits within a year.

Guidance
Falling in love can be akin to temporary madness!
If at all possible it is wise to live full time with your partner for at least a year without making any major life decisions such as marrying, having a child or entwining your financial affairs.

If after the love drug phase has passed (which, sadly, inevitably it will do) and you are still friends, care deeply for one another and can see past the foibles and annoying little habits of your loved one then the chances are that the relationship will be strong enough to endure.

Kate Figes, in her book *Couples: The Truth*, writes: 'The triumph of love lies in the small daily kindnesses and considerations which make one feel valued, seen and understood, not in the great romantic gushing gestures.'

However, human beings are unpredictable and one person's understanding of what true love means or how it is communicated can be at complete odds with another's. Beware the person who continually chases the thrills and highs of infatuation but who quickly tires of the 'small daily kindnesses'.

Love comes in all shapes and sizes and each of us will hold a personal view of what love means to us. There is parental love, love between siblings, love through friendship, sexual love, spiritual love, dutiful love, love that comes through shared religious, cultural or political values, love that endures through a lifetime of catastrophe or love that burns brightly and dies within months, love that insinuates itself in the hearts of the most unlikely of pairs, love born of the need for financial or emotional security. And then there is that most dangerous and pernicious kind of love: romantic, idealised love.

****

Romantic love is intoxicating but it tends to be ungrounded in reality. Think of how we are all bombarded on a daily basis with plays, songs, rom-com films, the ever-popular Mills and Boon books and reality TV programmes, all primarily concerned with romantic, unrealistic love.

The average wedding in the UK now costs around £25,000 and gone are the days when the bride's mother made the dresses and the reception for close family and friends was held in the local pub. The 'marriage industrial complex' has taken us over and with it the fantasy of what love and long-term relationships mean has become more and more detached from reality. It is even rumoured that prospective grooms are now hiring event companies to manage the proposal. How can the rest of day-to-day life compete with a choir appearing out of nowhere in Covent Garden to serenade us with our favourite song as our beloved sinks to one knee with a diamond ring in an outstretched hand?

A few years ago in a quiet London wine bar we overheard the following conversation between two thirty-something women.

'How is Kirsty?'

'Depressed, I think.'

And then without a trace of irony:

'Well, if you'd spent three years planning the wedding of your dreams I suppose six months after the day it's all a bit of an anti-climax really.'

'Yes, I suppose you are right.'

Poor Kirsty. But in truth we felt sorrier for Kirsty's new husband. The anticipation of the big day for Kirsty had obviously overshadowed the reality of day-to-day life but the truth is that most day-to-day life is pretty ordinary and a healthy and loving relationship should be able to accept that ordinariness and value it without anyone wanting to hold the other partner responsible for the lack of day-to-day glamour.

Guidance

Be realistic.

Are you in love with the idea of love, or a proposal or the idea of a big wedding?

Remember that the greater the romanticism and unrealism that surrounds a relationship the greater the anger and bitterness that will develop when, as is inevitable, reality comes a-calling.

There is also the danger that although we fall in love with someone, at some point we seek to change them.

'*When you love someone, you love the person as they are not as you'd like them to be*' —Leo Tolstoy.

Pretty words, Leo, but sometimes very difficult to follow.

Case Study

Gemma was three months into a six-month sabbatical from her job in the City of London when she met Brett on Bondi Beach. He was tall, bronzed, good-natured and a natural athlete – the stereotype of the 'surfer dude'. Brett worked at a water sports company. It was love at first sight for them both and he readily agreed to come back to London with her at the end of the holiday. Six months on Brett is getting ready to go back to Australia. After his tan faded and he found that he could only get jobs as a barman Brett became increasingly miserable, which was not helped by Gemma's insistence that he could retrain as an accountant's clerk. Gemma fell in love with an Adonis but really wanted to change him into a City worker and live a London commuter lifestyle.

****

How many of us have heard the words 'I'd love you more *if...*' If you were slimmer, prettier, more handsome, more ambitious, made more money, liked rock climbing...if, in other words, you were not you. If you are with a partner who regularly says this to you then run for the hills! No matter how much you diet, have cosmetic surgery to correct your physical imperfections or redouble your efforts to earn more money, we suspect that the spoken (or implied) '*if*' will always be there, which ultimately will not make you feel safe in that partnership.

***

In the course of our time together, no matter how deep our feelings are for each other we will deliberately or thoughtlessly hurt our partners. During our practice we would marvel at how forgiving people could be and it was rare that one act of infidelity or cruelty would trigger a divorce. It seemed to us that most people in love tended to overlook or forgive bad behaviour much more than we would tolerate in other relationships. However, most people did not forget and when the relationship had come to end it was amazing how many clients could recall so much detail of the hurt they had endured over many, many years.

In the 1970 film *Love Story* one line from the film launched a cliché – 'Love means never having to say you're sorry'- which must be the most ridiculous statement in movie history. In our experience those three little words, 'I am sorry', can clear away a lifetime of resentment and hurt and certainly should be practised on a day-to-day basis.

Guidance

Be a grown-up.

Do you hope that your partner will change in any way? Is this hope realistic?

Are you able honestly to admit your own mistakes and say sorry?

If you are on the receiving end of thoughtlessness or hurtful behaviour, are you able to voice your upset or do you silently seethe and feel resentful?

Remember seething resentment will slowly poison a relationship.

***

Communicating our love

We might feel love but we all have very different ways of communicating that love. It is important to understand how we show love for each other as a mismatch in styles can lead to deep distress.

Case Study

Olivia has been with her boyfriend, Tom, for two years. Tom is kind, attentive and very generous with his time and money. He often buys Olivia jewellery and takes her on wonderful holidays. However, Tom will not or cannot say to Olivia, 'I love you.' Olivia desperately needs to hear the words to feel secure in the relationship but when she asks Tom whether he loves her he simply smiles and shrugs. Tom feels that it should be obvious he loves Olivia from the amount of money and time he spends with her. Olivia is becoming more frantic in her attempts to get Tom to verbalise his feelings for her.

Dr Gary Chapman, in his book *The Five Love Languages*, writes that all of us perceive and express love differently. He feels that there are five main ways that we can communicate and feel loved and that problems arise when there is a mismatch in a couple's idea of how love is communicated. He says the five love languages are as follows:

1. Words of affirmation or love language
To feel that they are truly loved people like Olivia, above, need to actually hear the words 'I love you'. It does not matter that Tom is showing his love for her in presents and time spent with her. In fact, Tom would be better off saving his money and once in a while simply hugging Olivia and saying, 'I love you.'

2. Spending quality time together
Jefferson and Patrick have successful careers that demand lots of foreign travel. Neither feels the need for large romantic gestures or a verbalisation of their love and regard for each other but they both need the sanctuary and peace of their weekend home in the Kent countryside where they are able to spend hours together bird watching, walking and talking together. It is important to the couple to spend good quality time together whenever they can and this sustains their idea of a close, loving partnership.

3. Giving and receiving presents
Tom, above, showed his love and affection for Olivia through

gifts and taking her on expensive holidays but gifts do not need to be expensive or lavish for someone to feel loved. In fact, we saw many clients with enviable lifestyles, who stayed in five-star hotels, enjoyed extensive foreign travel, and owned several homes in various continents and who said, to our surprise, that they would willingly relinquish a lot of the material goodies for kind words or genuinely small loving gestures from their partner.

Sonia has been married to Bob for twenty-five years. Bob is a lorry driver for a company that delivers materials around Europe. Bob always brings Sonia a small gift back from his travels whether it be a bar of chocolate from Belgium or a knitting pattern from Normandy. Sonia feels that Bob is thinking about her when he is away from home, which makes her feel cherished and loved by him even though they spend little time together.

4. Physical touch

The need to communicate love through physical touch does not necessarily mean by sex and, indeed, someone who can only value a relationship through sex may not be communicating genuine love at all, just satisfying their own sexual itch. It sounds trite but an arm around a shoulder, a kiss, a daily hug or a fond and loving pat on the back can mean more to a person who needs physical touch to feel loved than any other form of communication.

Samantha likes her boyfriend, Ben, to hug her, hold her hand and generally be affectionate towards her as it makes her feel closer to him. Ben feels that any physical affection must lead to sex. Both feel frustrated with each other.

5. Acts of service to show support

Susan's mother is a no-nonsense Yorkshire woman who was left with three small children to bring up alone when her husband abandoned them. She is not given to words of love or sentiment and is most certainly not 'touchy-feely' with anyone. But Susan knows that if her mother visits she will clean her house for her and babysit the children without the need for any thanks. When Susan was ill her mother drove her to numerous hospital appointments.

Susan has the emotional maturity to recognise that her mother communicates her love and regard for her through these acts and Susan is grateful for that love despite her mother's lack of verbal or physical affection.

Guidance

Think about whether there is there a mismatch in how you and your partner show your love and regard for each other. Are you able to value the way your partner shows their love for you even if it is different from how you show your love and regard?

***

Expectations of life and love

From an early age we all have expectations of how our life will proceed. 'When I grow up I am going to be…' Fill in the blank. And when we get older we usually have firm expectations of how our emotional lives will run too. 'I want to be married by the time I am twenty-eight, have two children and run my own multimillion-pound business.' 'I want to be with someone who is rich and we will live in a penthouse in New York.' 'I'm going to be with a model, never have children and live in Marbella.' Funny, isn't it, that not many of us ever sits down and says, 'I want to marry someone I love and they love me, hopefully have children but definitely have a mortgage, and work hard to support my family', because how boring is that?

****

When we fall in love, don't all of us, if we are honest, not just fall in love with our partner for what they are but also to what extent they are fulfilling our expectations of how our life will play out in the future? And don't we have fixed expectations about how our loved one will treat us and demonstrate their love for us?

Susan, above, is very wise not to expect her mother to verbalise her love to her. Susan loves her mother for who she is and not what she expects her to be. So often a relationship flounders because the expectations of one or both partners can be unrealistic or just not flexible enough to accommodate any change that takes us away from our preconceived expectations. We have every right to hope that a relationship will fulfil our needs, whatever that means to us personally, but to expect anything else sets the bar way too high for many of us coping with our own emotions and the events that life throws at us.

Case Study
Peggy expected her partner, John, to earn enough money to run a large house, pay for private schooling for their three

children and maintain an expensive lifestyle with foreign holidays and flashy cars. In her eyes her expectations of the partnership were simple: John was lucky to have bagged a smart and attractive woman and Peggy should expect a comfortable lifestyle in return. When John lost his job in the downturn of 2008 it took him two years to find other employment at a vastly reduced salary. Peggy was furious and took every opportunity to berate, snipe or downright humiliate John. She had expected him to maintain a lifestyle for her even though she could not have provided it herself. Unsurprisingly, they have divorced and Peggy feels that she has somehow been cheated by John and life in general. Her bitterness has become all-consuming and the children have one by one gone to live with their father.

Peggy's unrealistic (and, frankly, heartless) expectation of the financial basis of her relationship with John outweighed any other factors in that relationship. No matter how good a father he is, how kind and supportive he has been to Peggy in the past or how well John provided for his family before being made unemployed, it all meant nothing to Peggy when faced with the disappearance of her inflexible expectation of somehow being 'owed' by John.

Case Study

Helen fell in love with Max because he was 'tall, dark and handsome'. 'Ugly men just don't do it for me,' she says. Max had been in the army and Helen also loved the feeling of physical security when she was with him. When Max was in a terrible car accident Helen was faced with a partner who had suffered permanent facial scarring and could not walk easily. Suddenly, Helen found that she could hardly bear to be with Max. She had not expected him to be so vulnerable and dependent on her or so permanently scarred, and when Max told Helen that he had fallen in love with one of the nurses who had helped him through his recovery all she felt was pure relief.

It would be easy to judge Helen harshly and to feel that if she had truly loved Max she would have stayed with him whatever had happened, but until we are tested by life how do we know how we would react? We would all like to think that 'love conquers all' and if we are very lucky we will not be tested by extreme life events.

**

So if love is the answer what are the questions you need to ask yourself? Remember when thinking about the following questions there are no right or wrong answers and you must try to be as honest as possible.

1.   What does the word 'love' mean to you?

2.   What do you think the word 'love' means to your partner?

3.   What does 'happiness' mean to you?

4.   Do you expect your partner to make you 'happy'?

5.   Do you feel that your partner makes you 'happy'?

6.   Do you feel that you make your partner 'happy'?

7. What hopes (or expectations) do you have about your relationship?

8. Are these hopes realistic?

9. How do you express your love to your partner?

10. How does your partner express their love to you?

11. Do you regularly argue or feel disappointed about how your partner expresses love to you or how you show love to your partner?

12. Do you regularly argue about or feel disappointed that your partner is not different in some way?

13. Do you have longstanding 'life goals' about lifestyle or the type of partner you should be with? How realistic are these goals?

If you have answered the above questions honestly, you will have taken the first steps to being able to take a more realistic view of your relationship. Realism may not have the same tantalising allure of gut-churning romanticism but, in our experience, it can save a lot of gut-wrenching agony later on.

"'I sometimes say – but not entirely seriously – that infatuation is the exciting bit at the beginning; real love is the boring bit that comes later," the poet Wendy Cope once told me."
— Stephen Grosz, *The Examined Life*.

Chapter Two
Self-awareness or know yourself: Part One

'This above all: to thine own self be true
And it must follow, as the night the day,
Thou canst not then be false to any man.'
—William Shakespeare

If we don't have some idea of who we are then how can anyone else know who we are and have a meaningful relationship with us? What has made us who we are?

We cannot expect our partner to know instinctively what we need to be a happy, fully functioning person and no one in a relationship should be expected to 'fix' another. If you have deep-seated emotional issues because of trauma, abuse or difficult life experiences, it is unfair and unrealistic to expect a partner to be able to deal with issues that are far beyond their knowledge or capabilities. If you were affected in your childhood by any of the following and are finding difficulty in sustaining close relationships in any area of your life, please seek out professional help (see the Resources section):

1. The death (particularly by suicide) of a parent or sibling
2. Any physical or sexual abuse suffered by you
3. The long-term sickness or disability of a parent or sibling
4. Abandonment by parent(s)
5. Severe mental health problems of a parent, sibling or yourself
6. Severe addiction problems – alcohol, drug, gambling, porn – of a parent, sibling or yourself

We are all a product of many things: genetic make-up; family history; the period of history we are born into; the social expectations of our society; our own indefinable personality quirks and traits; and our experiences (good or bad). A useful starting point into gaining insight into who we think we are is to consider the family we were raised in because our experiences of how we were raised will provide us with the lens through which we view the world and form a template for our future relationships.

Early experiences

'All parents damage their children. It cannot be helped. Youth like pristine glass, absorbs the prints of its handlers. Some parents smudge, others crack, and a few shatter childhoods completely into jagged little pieces beyond repair.' Mitch Albom, *The Five People You Meet in Heaven.*

How can that be? we ask ourselves. I am me and I am certain my family has had or has little influence over me. But think about it. If we had a happy, trouble-free childhood where all our emotional needs were met we will expect that to be replicated in our future adult relationships. We will have a low tolerance of bad behaviour within a relationship and are less likely to put up with such things as violence, addictions or infidelity by our partner.

Conversely, if we have had a less than perfect upbringing, perhaps taught by our early experiences that other human beings are neglectful, thoughtless or downright dangerous towards us, then, whether we reject our family of origin or not, its influence on us will be long-lasting. We may have a greater tolerance of neglectful, thoughtless or dangerous behaviour by our partner towards us because that it is what feels familiar to us, even when that behaviour can threaten our very sanity or physical safety.

Family

'They fuck you up, your mum and dad.
They may not mean to, but they do.
They fill you up with the faults they had
And add some extra, just for you.'
—Philip Larkin.

We all come into the world as helpless babies and our very survival, physically and emotionally, is entirely dependent on a committed caregiver, usually our mother and hopefully with the support of an interested father. None of us are born with a special handbook giving detailed instructions on how best we should be raised, but some of us have the misfortune to be born to parents who have absolutely no idea what is best for us.

Early trauma and neglect in childhood can lead us to a pessimistic attitude towards life, which will certainly affect our relationships in adulthood, and even if our childhood was free from actual abuse, life events can knock families off course, at the very least temporarily. Illness or death of a parent or sibling, divorce, mental health or addiction problems of a parent or sibling, unemployment and poverty or major outside events such as civil unrest or war can damage individuals within the family, with the effects spilling down the generations.

John Bowlby was an eminent psychiatrist and psychoanalyst who died in 1990. His idea of how our early experiences as children affect our ability to form secure and stable relationships throughout life, known as the 'theory of attachment', has been profoundly influential. In his 1988 book, *A Secure Base*, he wrote:

'...a central feature of my concept of parenting (is) the provision by both parents of a secure base from which a child or an adolescent can make sorties into the outside world and to which he can return knowing for sure that he will be welcomed when he gets there, nourished physically and emotionally, comforted if distressed, reassured if frightened.'

We are very lucky indeed if our parents have provided us with this secure base throughout our lives and if subsequently we can meet and form a relationship with someone who has also had such an upbringing.

Case Study

Callum is an only child from a stable and loving family. Jackie comes from a chaotic and noisy family where she was periodically beaten by her mother without any intervention from her often absent father. Callum met Jackie through work colleagues and was drawn to her lively wit and loud laughter. Jackie liked Callum's calm personality; she felt that he was her rock. They quickly moved in together and at first all went well but after a few months Callum became increasingly troubled by Jackie's mood swings and sulks.

Sometimes, Jackie would hardly speak for days and it was only after Callum's repeated attempts to understand what had gone wrong that Jackie explained that she regularly suffered flashbacks to the abuse she had suffered when she'd been a child. Callum tried to be calm and patient but after a year was drained and close to leaving. Jackie then became so panicked that was losing him that she made a half-hearted attempt at suicide. Thankfully, with the help of an understanding GP, Jackie was able to access counselling and instead of becoming silent when she is upset Jackie is now able to sit down with Callum and talk things through. Their relationship has survived.

***

The fact is that the manner in which our emotional needs have been met throughout our childhood will influence how we relate to others and, perhaps more importantly, how we relate to ourselves.

Scratch the surface of the history of many of us suffering emotional imbalance and it is probable that family dysfunction and disturbance will be at the root of it. However, that is not to say everyone born into a difficult family set-up is doomed to a life of chaotic or failed relationships.

Case Study

Terry and his two brothers were abandoned by their father after their mother's death when Terry was ten. The brothers were passed around various extended family homes until their maternal grandmother, Mary, took them in. She was very strict but the boys felt safe and protected in her care. Mary made sure that they were well-fed, clothed and attended school and, most importantly for Terry, she would tell them lovely stories about their mother. Terry admits that he and his brothers had the potential for petty crime in their teenage years but with great pride he talks about one brother who is now a policeman and the other who runs a successful car dealership. He himself is a tree surgeon and loves his work and his life with Sarah, his wife of fifteen years. Sarah is a loving and sympathetic woman and they have two children. Terry works hard to make sure he provides for his family and spends a lot of quality leisure time with them. Terry still finds it difficult to understand how his father could walk out on his family but simply says, 'That was him, not me. And that's that.'

Terry is lucky that he is able to transcend his difficult family circumstances and form a loving, stable family of his own. We all make a huge leap in emotional maturity when we are able to step back and see our parents for who they are. Not the all-powerful beings of our childhood but simply ordinary people with their own flawed understanding of the world who have come together and created us. They will have passed on their view of the world to us but in the long run we may have to reject their views, which do not fit with our perspective of life and how we wish to live that life.

****

Case Study

Barbara's mother came from a country riven by civil unrest and lack of respect for girls. Her mother came to the West with Barbara as a refugee and although was grateful for the educational opportunities and social freedom available to her she had a highly suspicious opinion of anyone she perceived to be an authority figure. Over time she developed mental health problems, a part of which was paranoia. When Barbara decided that she wanted to be a social worker her mother became convinced that Barbara was being trained to spy on her and after several very emotional scenes at home Barbara decided that the only way she could survive while she trained was to leave the family home and live with friends. At the moment Barbara does not have any emotional energy left over to invest in an emotional relationship and prefers to study and enjoy the company of her friends.

Barbara had the strength, the intelligence and, because she had good friends, the ability to break free of her mother's own assumptions about the world. Some of us are not as lucky as Barbara and no matter how hard we try, consciously or unconsciously, many of us cannot escape the 'family whisper', that little voice replaying the messages we were given in our childhood that cannot be silenced so easily. This is the voice that can either free us to enjoy our future life, experiences and relationships or hold us to ransom, shackling us to a past that frustrates our ambitions.

***

Case Study

Maria was brought up in an essentially loving and secure family but both her parents were heavily involved in a religious organisation that held a traditional view of heaven and hell. In her teenage years, much to the distress of her parents, Maria rejected her parents' faith. She moved out of the family home at eighteen to go to college and did not return to live there but maintained a friendly albeit distant relationship with her parents and siblings who were still committed to their faith. She has not told them that she has been living for several years with her partner, Julia. Although she feels secure in her relationship with Julia and the fact that she is gay, she suffers from periods of deep depression. No matter how hard she tries to rationalise her thoughts, it is difficult to stifle the voice of her parents telling her that hell awaits homosexuals.

Most of us come into the world craving unconditional love and regard but the family whisper can pass on very personal and critical messages to us that are difficult to ignore.

****

Who has not come across one or other of the following family statements at some point in their lives?
'You were always such a difficult child.'

'You were such a good baby.'
'You are the intelligent/stupid/pretty/handsome/ugly/ sporty/geeky one.'
'I never really wanted children so when you came along it was a shock.'
To a girl: 'We only wanted a boy.'
To a boy: 'We only wanted a girl.'
'You have always been a disappointment to us.'

These statements will inform our thoughts and again, consciously or unconsciously, will affect how we relate to others. Always been told you are an ugly little thing? It's very hard to feel attractive and desirable to anyone if you carry that undermining thought around with you. Always told you were clever and bright? You will expect others to value and respect your opinion and it's very unlikely you will lack self-regard. Always told you were worthless? Then, unless you are very lucky and have been able to disregard this message, it's likely you will attract partners who treat you as worthless.

Jon Kabat-Zinn is the founder of Mindfulness-Based Stress Reduction (usually called, simply, mindfulness), which has become increasingly popular worldwide. One of the central tenets of mindfulness is that our thoughts are not necessarily facts and practising mindfulness can help us disengage from our negative thoughts. It is possible to silence or at least disengage from the 'family whisper' but first you have to recognise what messages you were given.

Guidance

Think about any negative messages you were given as a child.

Now you are an adult how true are those messages?

How have those messages affected your choice of partner?

Does your partner reiterate any of those negative messages?

Case Study

Jessie was always told that she was the 'difficult one' in the family. She was the baby with colic who would not sleep, she was the child with dyslexia, she was the teenager with dyed hair and a tattoo and she was the one with the unsuitable boyfriends. Jessie had been given a label and felt compelled to fit the identity she had been given, and it got her a lot of attention from otherwise preoccupied academic parents. Jessie's parents were horrified when she announced that she had married Kyle in Las Vegas. Kyle is an itinerant musician with a fondness for drugs. The marriage only lasted a few months and if Jessie is honest she knew that it would break down quickly but her choice of Kyle helped to perpetuate her 'difficult' identity within the family, an identity that Jessie has begun to relish.

Even if it is not spoken out loud, the implied family message can be that love is conditional on achievement or behaving in a certain way.

***

Case Study

Barney was an only child of hard-working parents who owned a shop in central Birmingham. Barney's father had always regretted not having the opportunity to be educated at university level. Barney was a clever boy and always achieved good grades at school. It was very obvious to Barney that his parents were very proud of him and told their customers with great pride that Barney would go to Cambridge and eventually become a doctor. What Barney did not dare tell them was that he wanted to go to art college and although he was good at science-related subjects he hated studying them. When he once tried to voice his wish to become an artist his father did not speak to him for a week and his mother dissolved into tears every time she spoke to him.

As Barney was a 'good boy' and loved his parents, he decided to knuckle down and get into Cambridge, which he did. In his second year he began to have crippling panic attacks where he could not go to lectures. His girlfriend was struggling with her own workload and felt she could not support him. When they broke up Barney felt even more isolated. Barney has had to take a year out of his studies but still lacks the courage to tell his parents that he does not want to be a doctor. Barney also suspects that if he chose a partner who did not meet the approval of his parents, they would behave in exactly the same manner.

****

If we are told constantly by our family that there is a particular way to live our lives or that relationships with only certain types of people are possible if we are to be loved by them then when choosing long-term partners we may simply give in and concede that 'Mummy and Daddy know best' or may choose someone out of a knee-jerk reaction to annoy them. Neither method requires much thought and can equally cause us years of distress. Being self-aware requires us to think about why we choose or have chosen our partners.

The following questionnaire is intended to make you think about your family upbringing and the assumptions you may make and expectations that you may have of your close relationships because of that upbringing. Try to reflect on the questions and answer them as honestly as possible. Remember there are no right or wrong answers.

1. Did you feel loved unconditionally by your family?
2. Were your opinions valued and considered?
3. Did you feel that love was conditional on academic, material or other success?
4. Is one or both of your parents extremely critical of you and your life choices?
5. Were you assigned a role within the family – the good, bad, clever, stupid, etc., child? Do you continue to play into this stereotype in your relationship?
6. Do you have close sibling relationships?
7. Does it seem that one sibling has been preferred over you?
8. Did your family hold strict religious, political, educational or social beliefs that you do not share?

In reflecting on the above questions, does it occur to that you that in choosing a partner:

1. you are fulfilling (or have fulfilled) the expectations of your family, rather than fulfilling your own wishes and needs?
2. you have or are deliberately setting out to shock or frustrate the expectations of your family?
3. it is important to you (not your family) that your partner is the same religious, political, social class or educational background as you?
4. you are in a relationship where you are loved and valued unconditionally or does that love feel conditional? On what is it conditional?

***

Our wider family history

Family stories bounce down the generations, creating mythologies, particular belief systems and rigid family expectations, which, in turn, bizarre as it may seem, can affect our chances of successful relationships.

Case Study
Cindy's paternal great-great-grandmother married a member of the aristocracy and although any money or prestige from this marriage has long since gone, Cindy's father has been keen to impress on his children that marrying anyone lower than his perception of their social class would be a stain on the family honour. Every boyfriend Cindy brought home would be quizzed about his family background and dismissed on the basis he was not 'our sort'.

Cindy is now married to Geoff, who was born and brought up on a council estate but who is a successful businessman. Cindy's father can barely tolerate him and it means he sees little of his grandchildren, which Cindy feels is her father's loss. Thankfully, Geoff is very tolerant of his father-in-law, whose opinions have not caused any conflict between Cindy and Geoff.

Cindy's sister, Amanda, is not so lucky. She has viewed relationships through the prism of her father's lens and each boyfriend has been a disappointment – either financially successful without an acceptable background or with the required social class but financially unsuccessful. Amanda is unable to accept a boyfriend for who he is but is searching for an unattainable fantasy dictated by her father.

***

Case Study
Mary is an only child. Her grandmother had died in childbirth and Mary's mother had a very difficult pregnancy with Mary and decided not to have any more children after she was born. When Mary tried to have children with Ben, her partner, she found it impossible to conceive naturally, even though there was no physical reason why she could not.

Mary and Ben went through three rounds of IVF treatment and were able to have Sophie, a much wanted and adored child. However, the emotional and financial strain of having Sophie took its toll on the couple and they separated when Sophie was three. Looking back, Mary believes that the stories about childbirth handed down to her made her extremely fearful of pregnancy and that was a big part of why she had not conceived naturally.

Guidance
Think about your wider family history.
Are there family stories that repeat themselves through the generations? Do you feel any of these stories have affected you negatively or affected your choice of partner?

***

The attitudes of our generation

Each generation has its own core values and experiences. The post- war generation, known as 'Baby Boomers' (usually defined as those born 1946 to about 1964), have generally benefited from good economic conditions and in the main come from secure family backgrounds where divorce was not common. Generation X (born c.1965 to 1979) began to be affected by higher levels of family breakdown as divorce became easier and Generation Y or the Millenniums (born c.1980 to 1999) have experienced the loosening of many social, cultural and class inhibitions towards relationships. A recent study showed that the Millennium's biggest concern was happiness, not in terms of money or power but in love and friendship.

How we view the nature of relationships and what we expect from those relationships will necessarily change from generation to generation. Not many fathers in the 1950s attended the birth of their child, changed nappies or pushed prams. Until around the 1970s marriages between members of different social classes or cultures were rare, homosexuality was in the main socially unacceptable (and, indeed, a criminal act until 1967) and women were not equals to men at home or in the workplace. Thankfully, times have changed and there are now estimated to be around two million mixed-race children in the UK, a significant proportion of men take on full-time child care, same-sex marriages are now legal and women are not as bound by rigid expectations of gender at home or work.

Defining the core values and attitudes of different generations will, of course, involve generalisations but it's worth asking ourselves whether these values may have or had any impact upon our own personal relationships. It has been suggested recently that a high proportion of eighteen to twenty-five-year-olds report that they are bisexual. What if, for whatever reason, we feel out of step with the current attitudes of our generation? Will this hinder our chances of finding a long-term partner or will we feel pressured to go along with the presumed core values of our generation?

Case Study

Sue was twenty in 1976. She lived at home and worked locally in an office. She had been going out with her boyfriend, Perry, for two years when her mother found out that they had been sleeping together. Her mother was frantic and laid down an ultimatum: Sue had either to break up with Perry, marry him or never darken the family doorstep again. Sue and Perry married but the marriage lasted only three years and Sue's mother was once more distressed about the 'shame' of having a divorced daughter. Sue bitterly regrets allowing her mother to pressurise her into marriage but at the time she'd felt she'd had little choice. In the small town Sue was brought up in hardly anyone lived together and if they did it was called 'living in sin'.

It will seem ridiculous to later generations that Sue had to get married. Nowadays, of course, Sue would live with Perry, be able to test out the relationship and be able to move on with ease after the relationship had ended. But even with the freedoms afforded by more tolerant attitudes of the twenty-first century problems will still occur.

***

Case Study

Ruby was born in 1993. She left school after 'A' levels and is now happily working with a marketing firm on an apprenticeship scheme. She has lived with her boyfriend, Pete, for two years but has no thoughts of marriage or children. There is no family, economic or social pressure on her to marry Pete. Pete has told her that he would be happy to be a stay-at-home father if they did have children. However, Ruby's biggest concern is the number of hours Pete spends daily on social media and computer games rather than them spending time together. This causes arguments between them and Ruby is seriously questioning whether she should leave Pete. There is no family, social or economic pressure on Ruby to tolerate Pete's reluctance to spend more time with her.

Although the core values of our age group will usually play a lesser part in determining our choice of partner it is a fact that when (and also, obviously, where in the world) we are born will affect our expectations of those relationships.

Guidance
Think about how the core values of your age group affect your expectations of your relationships.
Do these core values conflict with your own personal or family values?

It is not easy being truly self-aware but thinking about aspects of our past, in our family upbringing, our family history and the society we have been brought up in can bring us closer to understanding our thoughts, actions and expectations in our intimate relationships. If we are able to become self-aware by honestly questioning what our part in our relationships is, we take huge steps towards emotional maturity and towards the possibility of leading deeper and more satisfying lives rather than being doomed to repeat our mistakes again and again. Rather than flailing around unconsciously reacting to the people and events around us we should be able to take stock, think and make conscious decisions based in reality rather than hope and fantasy. We do not need to take hold or pass on the family baton of dysfunction or unhappiness.

As Einstein is credited with saying: 'Insanity: doing the same thing over and over expecting different results.'

Chapter Three
Self-awareness or know yourself: Part Two

'It is said that adults who struggled with psychological problems as children…[are] less likely to marry, but if they do they are more likely to have partners who also earn less.'
—*The Times* (Monday, 16 March 2015)

Although our family, experiences and wider community play a major part in shaping our ideas of love and relationships, we are all born with innate characteristics that can help or hinder our chances of successful long-term relationships.

Annelli Rufus, a journalist and an author, writing in the *Daily Beast*, wrote about fifteen signs that could predict that a couple would divorce, one of which, on the face of it anyway, seems extremely odd.

'If you didn't smile for photographs early in life, your marriage is *five* times more likely to end in divorce than if you had smiled intensely in early photographs.' (authors' emphasis)

The obvious and short conclusion that we can draw from this point is that fundamentally happy and cooperative people are more likely to form long-lasting relationships. No one, unless they have masochistic tendencies, begins a relationship hoping that their partner will be difficult, unfaithful, bad-tempered, critical, an alcoholic, a drug addict, abusive, violent, a bankrupt or a liar. We all have a shadow side to our personality but some of us have darker and bleaker aspects to our personalities, which will inevitably hinder the success of relationships.

Psychologists often refer to the 'Big 5' traits when looking at personality types. Although we acknowledge that human personalities do not often fit neatly into simple categories, it is worth considering the traits as conflict within our relationships is often caused by our differing personality types.

1. Openness to experience

Openness to experience can be interpreted in a number of ways. How open are we to new ideas, adventure or of a lack of routine? How imaginative or intellectually curious are we?

'We had fun playing house at first, using our new cappuccino maker and make-your-own pizza kit, and sliding into bed together every night…But after six months of the reality of marriage (after five years of the surreality of long-distance dating), I grew conscious of, or actually paid attention to, our differences. I loved to read, study, go running, lie in the sun on summer Saturdays, work hard, make money, travel. He

didn't. He liked to play sports and watch TV and hang out with his family.'

H. K. Brown (*'Yanking Tulips' from Ask Me About My Divorce*, edited by Candace Walsh)

***

Case Study

Josh and Lizzie met in their early twenties through a shared love of surfing. Lizzie likes high-adrenaline sports, including heli-skiing, snow-boarding and rock climbing. Lizzie sees her future working for six months of the year to accumulate enough money to travel and pursue her love of extreme sports. While initially Josh found this lifestyle exciting, he now wants to buy a house and settle down to have a family. Lizzie has no intention of 'rotting in a semi for the rest of her life'. Lizzie constantly seeks new thrills and will not compromise her life for Josh. They have now decided to separate.

Case Study

Peter and Naomi have been together for nine months. Peter loves going to the theatre, museums and exhibitions. Naomi prefers shopping and hanging out in wine bars, chatting to friends and 'having a laugh'. In Peter's eyes Naomi has no intellectual curiosity at all and it is becoming obvious to them both that each is bored with the other despite the fact this is a relatively new relationship.

****

2. Conscientiousness: how dependable, dutiful or ambitious are we?

It's a fact of human nature that some of us are highly disciplined, conscientious and/or ambitious in our emotional and work lives and some of us are not.

Case Study

Charlotte's personal mantra was, 'What will be, will be.' In the early days of her relationship with Andy he loved Charlotte for her calm and relaxed attitude towards life. Andy was brought up in an army family where duty and discipline were seen as the keys to a successful life. After two years together Charlotte's lack of ambition and her passivity began to irritate Andy more and more and although on paper, at least, they had many other things in common, Andy eventually left Charlotte for a work colleague who was equally driven in her ambition to succeed.

***

3. Extrovert (or introvert)

Extroverts tend to love socialising, finding the stimulation of new people, new ideas and discussion highly energising. Introverts tend to seek more solitary activities and although they can be seen as 'loners' are usually happy with their own company or being with a few people at a time. In extreme cases extroverts and introverts with their polar opposite views of socialising will make each other very unhappy (if indeed they manage to get together in the first place!). We found that problems with differing ideas of socialising often came when the business or work of one partner demanded that the other attend business-related functions.

Case Study

Amy was married to Bill. She was the marketing manager of a large company that relied on networking to generate business. Amy loved her career and had to attend client dinners or social events and would often ask Bill to come with her. Bill hated attending these functions, which he felt were superficial and false and where he found great difficulty in talking to large groups of new people. Amy felt that Bill's refusal to support her showed a lack of respect for her work, which after all brought in a healthy income that allowed them to send their children to private schools and pay for expensive family holidays. Bill felt that his very soul was under attack. Neither could understand the position of the other.

***

4. Agreeableness. How cooperative or compassionate are we? How willing to compromise are we?

Being willing to cooperate or compromise is not code for 'How willing are you to be a doormat?' It is the ability to see the other's side and decide how significant the potential argument is to us. An ability to speak our minds and resolve conflict without resorting to screaming arguments or violence is a sign of a healthy relationship. A rigid or inflexible approach to life or relationships usually does not leave much room for love and affection within them.

Case Study

Tony's favourite saying was, 'I don't suffer fools gladly.' Once he had made up his mind about the rights or wrongs of any situation he took great pride in maintaining his position come what may. He felt that compromise was just another word for 'giving in'. It seems to have escaped his notice that because of his inflexible and bullish attitude he has been divorced three times. Tony might remember that to be loved we usually have to be loveable and there is nothing loveable about a tyrant.

***

5. Neuroticism: or how stable emotionally are you?

Are you able to take the good and the bad of life and respond to events and circumstances in a balanced manner? Or are you a mass of phobias, contradictory emotional states, an all-or-nothing personality bound up with a rigid expectation of the world and relationships?

Case Study

Victoria is an attractive woman in her thirties with a successful career in the media. She has no difficulty attracting men but none seem to stay around for more than a few months or so. Victoria cannot understand why friends she considers less successful than her and not as attractive as her are with long-term partners. She was astounded when her last boyfriend, the man whom she thought she would settle down with, told her that he could not stand her screaming rages if they went to a restaurant or on outings when things did not go exactly to plan. He told Victoria that he felt he was constantly on edge anticipating her moods – it was like living on the edge of a volcano. Victoria has always been proud of her exacting standards – after all this is what has made her so successful in her career – but unfortunately it is the very thing that has pushed away potential partners. Victoria seems incapable of understanding that she is just too difficult to be around.

We sometimes forget that a partner has chosen to be with us (and we with them) and that no matter how complicated the emotional or financial entanglements we have with them, no matter how many children we have created together or how many promises we have made to each other about staying together through 'sickness and in health, till death do us part', if it all gets too difficult a partner can walk or run away, temporarily or permanently.

***

In our experience couples tend to forget four basic things in a relationship – Appreciation, Affection and Good Manners and Kindness. A simple thank you and a hug for our partner for doing the shopping, DIY jobs around the house, doing the school run, bringing a cup of tea in bed or listening to the work woes of the day may sound woefully trite but feeling undervalued and underappreciated in a relationship can undermine the best of us. The drip-drip-drip of criticism over years leads to the erosion of self-confidence and no matter how great the sex, what amazing holidays were enjoyed or what material successes were shared, we heard many divorce clients bemoan the fact that a basic lack of regard and kindness from a partner had made them feel belittled and overlooked or, worse, that their confidence had been completely undermined.

Case Study

Lily and Sam met at sixth-form college and have been together for three years. They are both bright, intelligent twenty-year-olds and chose to study at the same university, although they live in separate halls of residence. Sam is constantly critical about Lily's new friends, her choice of clothes and music and her views on politics. Lily thinks she loves Sam and when they are together he is generally fine – as long as she is doing what he wants. Despite it being obvious to anyone around her that Sam is trying to control Lily, she is finding it hard to finish the relationship; university is exciting but scary and Sam is a strong, reassuring presence. But even after only three years Sam's lack of respect for Lily is beginning to undermine her confidence about her views, looks and her ability to succeed in the world without him. Fast-forward fifteen years and we suspect Lily will be a sad shadow of her former self.

Having good manners sounds very old-fashioned but we found that courtesy could help oil the wheels of many a creaking relationship. Constant swearing, shouting, belching or farting does not a lady or a gentleman make! Courtesy really comes down to your awareness of the other person in the relationship and your attempt to treat them with respect.

****

Man at dinner party to fellow diner: 'What do you think is important in a relationship?'

Fellow diner: 'A shared sense of humour and the feeling you are "on the same side", and respect and appreciate each other, I suppose.'

Man (in anger): 'What [expletive] Milly-Molly-Mandy books have you been reading?'

Fellow diner: 'Obviously, not the same ones you've been reading because I'm still married and you've been divorced twice!'

End of conversation.

****

We live in a highly competitive society ever more driven by results in education, jobs, wealth creation and even in our choice of partner. It seems to us that the word 'kindness' has become a dirty one. If you admit to being a kind person you might as well say that you are a failure.

Case Study

Jocelyn is a goal-driven, highly ambitious businesswoman in her mid-forties. She is married to Del and has three children aged between ten and sixteen years-old. Jocelyn schedules her family life as she schedules her business life, with every minute allocated to a specific task. The children are expected by her to achieve high grades at school and Del to provide a level of income equivalent to her own. Recently, Del has had a few periods of illness resulting in hospital admissions and Jocelyn told him in no uncertain terms that she would be unable to visit him regularly as her business meetings had first priority.

Del has told Jocelyn that he wants a trial separation. He says he is exhausted by their regimented lifestyle and has been deeply wounded by the lack of kindness and thought she has shown him while he has been ill. Jocelyn's immediate response was, 'Kind people are not winners.' Del is not sure what personal race Jocelyn is running but he is coming to the conclusion that he is not prepared to participate any longer.

****

We should all be bringing the best of ourselves to a committed relationship but all too often it becomes the dumping ground for bad behaviour. We can have been with our partner for years but if we do not feel valued by them or we feel that we are simply fulfilling the sexual needs of our partner without any true affection or desire, or we are treated rudely and with contempt, we will feel demeaned and resentful, both of which are toxic emotions. If we feel demeaned by or resentful towards anyone we tend to behave in one of two ways: with returned aggression or martyrdom, neither of which contribute to a healthy relationship.

Guidance
Do you feel a perpetual feeling of resentment towards your partner?
Can you remember what started these feelings of resentment?
Have you tried to address your feelings with your partner or are you playing the 'martyr'?

The more the balances and checks of our emotional life are able to keep us stable the more at ease we will be with ourselves and others. However, quirks and eccentricities can add to the appeal of a character and certain areas of life seem to produce greater instability than others without being valued less by us. Think rock stars, writers, poets and artists, many of whom share a high degree of neuroticism but with a high degree of creativity – not that many tend to have wonderfully stable long-term relationships but no doubt are very exciting to be with in the initial stages!

Although in our practice as divorce lawyers we saw many relationships come unstuck because of conflicting core personality traits, we also saw that more seemingly mundane characteristics could cause high degrees of tension in a relationship.

These were:
1. *Timekeeping*
2. *Being excessively untidy or tidy*
3. *Hobbies*

1. Timekeeping
'I have noticed that the people who are late are often so much jollier than the people who have to wait for them.'
— Edward Verrall Lucas

Whether chronic bad time keeping is a lack of self-discipline, a conscious effort to control a person, an event or expectation or a symptom of just trying to fit too many things into the day, the effect on the punctual partner can be explosive. At the beginning of the 'love drug' phase we may be inclined to excuse bad timekeeping in a partner as charmingly eccentric, lovably ditzy or confirmation that our partner's time is more valuable than ours. However, as a relationship progresses and trains and planes are missed, the beginnings of films and plays are never seen and friends smile grimly as they wait to order food at the restaurant then bad timekeeping can be seen as highly disrespectful, impolite and, depending on how many times you've missed the plane, very expensive. 'Compromise' should be the key word here.

Case Study

Laurence and Paul have been together for twenty years. Laurence, an accountant, is habitually early for all appointments, whether work or socially related. Paul, a journalist, is always late. Laurence used to spend many hours fuming while waiting for Paul to show up to the cinema, art exhibitions or airports. Paul's lateness was like a running sore in their otherwise compatible existence. Laurence then hit on the idea of leaving any tickets for Paul at the box office and they travelled to airports or train stations separately. Over the years Paul has made an effort to be on time for more things but because Laurence has stopped trying to change Paul into an efficient timekeeper like himself Laurence has found that his own stress levels have decreased.

However, major problems can occur if the habitual lateness is being used as an attempt to control or deliberately annoy the other partner.

Guidance

Are you using habitual lateness as a deliberate ploy to punish your partner in some way?

Or are you using the habit as an attention-seeking device on the basis that any attention (good or bad) from your partner is better than none? Do you suspect your partner is using lateness to deliberately annoy or control you?

If a practical compromise has not been possible and bad timekeeping is becoming a major stumbling block in your relationship then it is possible professional couple therapy would be appropriate, at whatever stage you happen to be within your relationship.

2. Excessive tidiness or untidiness

'Some are stifled by excessive tidiness while others feel oppressed by mess to the point where they cease to be able to function.' — *'The Shrink and the Sage: Does Tidiness Matter?'* by Antonia Macaro and Julian Baggini, 27 September 2013 (*FT Magazine*)

We commonly associate untidiness with creativity, which is fine if we are a modern-day Picasso or Virginia Woolf but can be extremely irritating if we are not and it seems to our partner that we simply cannot be bothered to pick up our own mess; somehow the dirty pots and pans in the kitchen and clothes strewn around the bedroom become a visible symbol of our contempt for the other. On the other hand, our tidy partner's need to keep chaos at bay at all times can stretch our nerves to breaking point – what is wrong with a little temporary mess?

The only way we are able to compare our attitudes to tidiness is to live together and once again be open to compromise, otherwise this mundane topic can become a running battleground throughout the relationship, with the danger you can turn into 'the naughty child' or the 'nagging parent'. We were often surprised at the number of arguments between partners we were told about that centred around washing and tidying up the kitchen; invariably one partner could not bear to leave a mess overnight after supper/ dinners or parties while the other could not care less.

Case Study

Judy and Paul have been married for thirty years. Paul is extremely untidy and Judy, although not a fanatic, likes a tidy home. After many, many disputes about dirty clothes being strewn around their bedroom a compromise has been reached. An invisible line has been drawn down the middle of the bedroom. On one side order reigns and on the other chaos has won. Each agrees not to comment on the other's tidiness/untidiness and each has agreed not to encroach on the space of the other.

However, if the need for tidiness has become an obsessive compulsion or, indeed, if untidiness has tipped into a lack of regard for one's personal/home's cleanliness then it maybe that professional help should be sought as both could be (although not always) a sign of depression.

Guidance

As with timekeeping, our attitudes to tidiness/untidiness can be open to interpretation by our partner.

Is it a method to deliberately annoy or control the other? Is it a deliberate policy of contempt? What compromises can we make?

3. Hobbies

There are hobbies and there are hobbies! A shared love of bird watching, travel, Civil War reconstructions, paintballing, sailing and so on can strengthen and add joy to any relationship. A hobby can add interest and broaden our experience of the world, even if it is following Manchester United to all their away fixtures. But what if the hobby takes up hours of spare time away from us or our partner and/or costs a lot of money to maintain?

Case Study

Delia lived with Michael for four years but in the end decided to end the relationship. Michael spent hours every night and at the weekend glued to the computer screen, playing an online fantasy game. When they first met Delia did not mind too much as she worked long hours during the week and at weekends Michael did not make a fuss if she wanted to socialise with her friends. The crunch came when Delia realised that Michael was also spending lots of his income on virtual money to spend within the game. Not only was their time together limited but Michael had no spare cash for holidays or any other form of entertainment. Delia felt that they had become like flatmates and when she tried to talk to Michael about her concerns he was just not interested.

Case Study

Rosie is in her twenties, and adores Harry. Harry's abiding passion is rock climbing and most weekends and holidays he wants them to rock climb. If they travel he finds the nearest mountain and expects Rosie to climb with him. At first it was exciting but after three serious falls, the last one where she broke her arm, Rosie is becoming increasingly terrified of climbing. Rosie is in a dilemma – does she not spend as much time with him so he can climb with his club and other friends or does she share his passion and stick with it? It seems a pity to give up on the relationship when they get on so well on a day-to-day basis but Harry has made it clear he has no intention of giving up his hobby. Does Rosie simply accept the non-negotiable aspect to Harry's character?

Guidance

A conscious acceptance and a willingness to tolerate each other's traits will help a relationship but, and it is a big but, acceptance and tolerance does not mean always passively giving in.

As we will see from Chapter Four, conflict in a relationship is unavoidable and sometimes necessary. It is how you handle that conflict that will determine the success of any relationship.

We are not advocating that we should all try to adopt a false happy-clappy approach to life and relationships. It is inevitable that at different times in our lives and at different stages of our relationships we will be happier than others.

But once again, if we are to be self-aware it is important to understand how we present ourselves to others. It is a fact that unless you have other compensating features (think the eighty-year-old multimillionaire with the twenty-five-year-old blonde bombshell wife), if you are a bad-tempered pessimist with addiction problems then you are unlikely to be seen as the best candidate for a long-term, mutually rewarding relationship. Like most of us, you will have good and bad days, days when you moan and lose your temper, days when all you want to do is pull the bedclothes over your head and forget the world and your responsibilities.

But don't forget, just as you are supremely human so is your partner and a little appreciation, affection, kindness and good manners go a very long way in ensuring your relationship for the most part stays on track.

Chapter Four
Conflict

*'Usually when people are sad they don't do anything.
They just cry over their condition. But when they get
angry, they bring about change.'*
—Malcolm X

When we fall in love not many of us want to accept that arguments and discord will be part of our continuing relationship. Surely soulmates agree on everything? Of course, we all know individuals and couples who seem to thrive on the drama of flaming rows and passionate reunions; they are the 'cats and dogs' of the relationship world, blithely racking up the emotional agony and leaving on-looking family and friends exhausted and for the most part bemused. On the whole the Taylor/Burton diva method of relationship conflict, with or without the diamonds, leaves us cold and rationally we should agree with author Jules Evans in his book *Philosophy for life. And other dangerous situations:*

'There is something spoilt, infantile and ungrateful about anger. We kick and scream like a child when the world does not immediately adopt our "king's point of view".

Dealing with conflict

Perversely it seemed to us that the presence of anger and disagreement between couples is necessary to keep a relationship energised and moving forward. We saw that indifference between partners usually heralded the death knell of the relationship a good deal quicker than relationships that had higher levels of conflict in them.

If we saw a client shrug a shoulder, sigh and say, 'What can I do? There is no point in arguing,' it was a sure sign someone had checked out of the relationship and had neither the will nor desire to maintain it no matter what the financial or practical consequences might be.

Dr John Gottman and his wife, Dr Julie Schwartz Gottman have spent nearly forty years scientifically studying and researching relationships. They say, *'...relationship conflict is natural and has functional, positive aspects.'*

By conflict we do not mean violence (either physical or verbal), where one party seeks to control, intimidate or subjugate a partner. Neither does it include those among us who use the heightened charge of conflict or actual violence to pep up a flagging sex life.

'Hugh and I have been together for so long that in order to arouse extraordinary passion we need to engage in physical combat. Once, he hit me on the back of the head with a broken wine glass, and I fell to the floor pretending to be unconscious. That was romantic, or would have been had he rushed to my

side rather than stepping over my body to fetch the dust pan.'
— David Sedaris, *Dress Your Family in Corduroy and Denim*

Possible deal-breakers

In any relationship there will be 'deal-breakers' where behaviour or attitudes of one of the partners will create conflict at so great a level that at some point someone will say, 'Enough,' and the relationship will be lucky to survive. In our experience, deal-breakers are unique to each relationship. Different couples will place a different emphasis on what constitutes behaviour that will end the relationship. One act of infidelity can crush the life out of one partnership, whereas others may tolerate numerous instances of unfaithfulness. An often-quoted statistic shows that many women tolerate around thirty-five incidents of violence at the hands of their partner before they decide to report this abuse yet for another, one act of violence will not be tolerated even after many years together. Drug, alcohol, sex and gambling addictions or criminality can be looked on with horror or dismissed as part and parcel of a long life, lived dangerously but with interest.

****

Elisabeth Luard was married to her husband, Nicholas, for forty years. Her account of their long marriage in her book, *My Life as a Wife*, is succinctly summarised on the jacket sleeve.

Luard's fascinating, witty and often brave memoir charts forty years of marriage to a man who was as cavalier and unreliable as he was charismatic and charming. Good looking and athletic, with a keen intelligence and a deep understanding of and love for woman, Nicholas Luard was also an absentee father, a philanderer, a wheeler dealer whose numerous harebrained business schemes usually lost rather more than made money, and ultimately a man whose love of the bottle was all-consuming. But while life with Nicholas was never going to be easy, it was also never going to be dull.

For many of us there would be any amount of deal-breakers in the Luard marriage but it endured for forty years, until Nicholas's death.

For those starting out on a committed relationship a lack of sex in a long-term relationship might be seen as a deal-breaker but funnily enough it never seemed to us to be a deal-breaker, just symptomatic of a diminishing level of intimacy that only with a combination of other factors might in the end finish off the relationship.

Leaving aside deal-breakers (which we will come back to later on in the book) that can end a long-term partnership overnight, we saw that on the whole it was more the continuing small annoying habits, irritating characteristics and petty acts of thoughtlessness or lack of regard that, if not challenged, will over time vastly erode and undermine the quality of a relationship.

The Gottmans' research seems to show that defensiveness, stone-walling and criticism will cause trouble in relationships but adopting a contemptuous attitude towards our partner (or they towards us) will be the most destructive force. A common complaint we heard regularly from our clients was that the contemptuous attitude of a partner had thoroughly undermined their confidence.

The lesson here seems to be that we should not allow ourselves to be treated in a careless, thoughtless or downright rude way by our partner and that any such behaviour should be immediately challenged to clear the air and enable us to move on without holding on to resentment or bitterness.

Guidance
Start as you mean to go on!
If you are starting a new relationship with potential for long-term commitment the lesson is even clearer. If you allow an unhealthy dynamic to begin, it will only get worse in time not better.

And so in an ideal world we should be able to sit down and have a one-to-one chat (or scream) with our loved one to deal with disagreements or challenge our partner's upsetting behaviour. However, not everyone deals with or responds to the threat of conflict in a calm, sensible and rational manner and couples tend to develop 'no-go areas' of discussion that, if left unresolved, can easily turn into suppurating bitterness or contempt. In lots of relationships, for many and varied reasons, it simply does not feel safe to express or challenge anger, disappointment or upset and so the years roll by until either a partner leaves the relationship either emotionally or physically or becomes ill or depressed. Do not underestimate the corrosive and destructive potential on a relationship or an individual of not expressing anger.

Case Study

Tania is in a civil partnership with Susie. Tania is a cool-headed head teacher of a troubled inner-city secondary school. Susie is an artist who is not unsuccessful but does not have Tania's earning power or confidence. Susie tends to defer to Tania in discussions about politics, religion and education, subjects that do not really interest her. Susie takes care of all domestic matters, including being responsible for their social life. In front of friends Tania refers to Susie as her 'house-elf' and on occasions if they are entertaining at home will click her fingers and shout, 'House-elf, bring me a drink.' At first this seemed amusing but over the years Susie has begun to feel more and more demeaned by Tania, who has become more and more critical of Susie (in private and in public) and has also been known to pat Susie on the head in front of people and call her 'my silly wifey'. If Susie tries to challenge Tania about her behaviour Tania adopts her 'headmistress voice' and tells Susie that she is generally useless and is lucky to be in a relationship with such a high-achieving partner. Susie is finding that she often feels tearful and is having difficulty concentrating on her work, which compounds her feelings that Tania is probably right about her general uselessness. She is in danger of slipping into depression.

****

During our time as divorce lawyers we saw many clients who had experienced different kinds of conflict within their relationships. Some had been the instigators of conflict and some had borne the brunt of the destructive behaviour of their partner. Behaviour (not of the deal-breaker kind) that can provoke conflict includes constant criticism, passive/aggressive comments, usually under the guise of teasing, lack of regard or respect for the other's views or wishes, bullying, belittling or threatening words and, interestingly, playing the martyr – it's difficult to challenge someone who has decided they are the victim, even if their behaviour is appalling.

Guidance
In our dealings with clients we saw that on the whole it was how couples dealt with conflict in their relationship rather than what they argued about that determined whether the relationship would necessarily end in a separation or divorce.

We saw that the way individuals dealt with conflict seemed to be influenced by either how they had experienced conflict in their own childhood or their particular temperament or, on many occasions, whether there was an imbalance emotionally or financially within the relationship. The latter category is probably the most difficult for couples to deal with, particularly if young children are involved or if one party to the relationship is economically more dependent on the other.

Case Study
Eleanor and Ben met at university and married in their mid-twenties. They have fun and generally get on well. Eleanor, however, does not like arguing. At the first sign of an argument Eleanor will burst into tears and on occasions

leave their flat. Ben feels that this 'drama queen' behaviour is unacceptable. 'I only mentioned that it was irritating that she forgot to put out the rubbish last week. Why the tears?'

Eleanor has not told Ben that when she was young any arguments between her parents meant smashed plates and broken furniture. On one occasion when her mother left the house her father told Eleanor and her sister that they'd have to go into care if their mother did not return. Her parents are still together and now laugh about this troubled period in their marriage. Eleanor, however, equates conflict with potential abandonment and finds it difficult to stay around Ben if she feels trouble is brewing.

Case Study

Jasmine and Dexter have been together for two years. Dexter is a personal trainer and is proud of his physique and strength. Jasmine is a nurse and has been having difficulty controlling her weight after a year of night shifts when sugary drinks and treats kept her alert at night. Dexter makes no attempt to hide his disdain for Jasmine's weight gain. He prods her around the waist and stomach, saying, 'Too many burgers.' But when Jasmine becomes cross with him Dexter retreats from an argument by saying, 'I was only joking. You are so touchy.' Jasmine seethes with frustration. However, she is temperamentally unsuited to his passive/aggressive approach and is preparing to tell Dexter the relationship is over.

Case Study

Judith and Mark have been together for fifteen years and have three children aged six to thirteen. Judith is, by her own admission, 'a bit of a bully'. She is attractive, well-educated and four inches taller than Mark and, although it is not articulated by him, Mark feels lucky to have attracted Judith. If Mark dares to challenge Judith about anything she becomes very red in the face, stands very close to him and shouts extremely loudly and aggressively, usually about how weedy and pathetic he is. This upsets Mark and the children greatly.

There is an obvious imbalance in Mark and Judith's relationship. He feels lucky to be with Judith and he is worried about upsetting the children any further. Mark is always slightly on edge that Judith will up sticks with the children and that he will be left on his own. After all, in his eyes, 'Who would be idiot enough to take on someone like me?' Although Mark refuses to openly challenge Judith on things about her behaviour that upset him, there is often an air of tension in the house and the eldest child often suffers from bad migraines. It might be better for the family as a whole if Mark would challenge Judith and suffer the consequences if there is a major argument.

****

Time and time again when talking to our clients one of the most common complaints we heard was how humiliated and worthless they were made to feel over the course of the relationship by their partner. Openly sneering and contemptuous remarks can be as painful as physical blows and can create a simmering hostile environment but one that is often difficult to escape. The longer we are with partners and build up complicated emotional histories, family structures, financial entanglements and dependencies, the easier it is to become trapped in an unhealthy conflict dynamic and the harder it is to deal with bad behaviour emanating from your partner. If you have nothing to lose in the early stages of a relationship, no children, no financial entanglements or no family expectations, then it is much easier to walk away; not so easy if you have been together for twenty-five years, with several children and you are partially or wholly dependent (either financially, emotionally or because of illness) on your partner.

****

Not only may we be inhibited in dealing with conflict because we feel trapped by emotional or financial constraints, it may be that our partner's way (or our own way) of dealing with or avoiding potential conflict can undermine or block the potential for the healthy resolution of disagreements. It comes down to: what is your partner's (or your) style of arguing?

Is your partner or you:

The Nuclear Over-reactor?
At the first hint of disagreement voices are raised to a shout or scream, faces are contorted, hands are waved and every grievance over the last twenty years is rehashed, whether or not it is relevant to the dispute under immediate discussion. The words 'You always (insert allegations of perceived bad behaviour)' will be shouted a lot. This is a very effective

method of squashing any possibility of resolving issues sensibly and will usually push any contentious matters underground, although these will inevitably emerge at a later date unless, of course, the less volatile partner has enough of the histrionics and decides to leave the relationship. If you are both 'nuclear over-reactors' then the chances of arguments escalating to physical violence are high.

Tina is an attractive twenty-eight-year-old with a volatile temper who at the first sign of trouble will open the kitchen cupboards and throw plates to the floor. 'I am passionate,' she says with a smile. Her previous boyfriends don't agree and more than one has interpreted the passion as madness before he hurried for the front door, never to return!

The Ostrich?

Having a head-in-the-sand approach to conflict will not necessarily ensure a calm relationship. If we seek to avoid conflict at any cost and adopt a placatory or passive role, sooner or later our partner will assume a more dominant role in the relationship. Inevitably, at the very least we will be taken for granted; at its worst we will be treated with contempt and derision. 'The ostrich' approach encourages the bully so don't be surprised if at some stage this method of avoiding conflict puts you in the position of the victim.

Brian and Tamsin have been together for forty years and are retired. Brian is the epitome of the stereotype 'henpecked husband' and Tamsin's desires, wishes and demands are always met with agreement by Brian, even though he often does not agree and has spent a lot of time harbouring almost murderous thoughts about Tamsin throughout the marriage. For whatever reason, Brian has never had quite the courage to stand up to her. Sadly, Brian had a major stroke a few months ago and to Tamsin's immense distress has told the hospital that he does not want her to visit him. Brian has told Tamsin that once he recovers (if he recovers) he will not be returning to their home. Tamsin is astounded and has no idea that forty years of resentment have been uncovered by Brian's illness.

The Bolter?

In *The Pursuit of Love* by Nancy Mitford, the narrator's mother is called 'The Bolter' for her habit of leaving a trail of relationships and marriages behind her when things were not to her liking. Within relationships 'the bolter' will deal with conflict by immediately exiting through the door at the first sign of trouble, sometimes not returning for days on end. Mary was the child of a very unhappy marriage and made a solemn pact with herself that she was never going to endure such unhappiness in her own marriage. So, unbeknown to her husband, Martin, she kept a packed suitcase under the bed and, of course, it was all too easy to use it when any conflict arose, although she always returned after a few days. 'The bolter' method of conflict resolution will provoke high levels of frustration within the other partner and can poison and strain the atmosphere in the home for any unfortunate third party (usually the children) living in the house.

The Martyr?

In *Enchanted April* by Elizabeth Von Arnim, her character Mrs Arbuthnot is described as having 'the face of a patient and disappointed Madonna', which is a vivid image of 'the martyr': a person who will use their past or present suffering to stifle disagreements or, indeed, themselves behave with impunity either inconsiderately, rudely or downright badly. The implied or vocalised message is, Who could possibly argue with me or find fault with me? Me, who has suffered or is suffering so much?

Maybe currently 'the martyr' is very ill, or has had a serious illness, or maybe they have suffered past abuse. Or, just maybe, their partner has been guilty of past misdemeanours (particularly infidelity), which 'the martyr' has, of course, forgiven but cannot quite resist mentioning when the possibility of disagreement raises its head.

It's difficult to argue with 'the martyr', who seeks to use their status as a self-styled victim to avoid criticism or conflict, but unless you wish to cast yourself in a masochistic role, dancing attendance on 'the martyr's' every wish, then you must set boundaries and stop feeling sorry for or guilty about them.

Samantha has been with Rob for three years. At the beginning of their relationship Samantha had an ill-judged one-night stand after an office party, which foolishly she told Rob about. Rob was extremely upset but after a few weeks of indecision told Samantha that he loved her too much to let this one indiscretion ruin their relationship, and Samantha was overjoyed that he had forgiven her. Or had he? Every time they argue Rob manages to hint that because he has forgiven Samantha's past bad behaviour she cannot expect to challenge him on any matter. Because Samantha still feels guilty about the one-night stand she is, in effect, a hostage in this relationship.

The Concrete Wall?

'The concrete wall' style of arguing is as infuriating as it is inflexible. It comes down to 'I am right. You are wrong.' There is no moving anyone who adopts this stance and you either fall in with their view of life and how it should be lived or leave. Although this attitude can be very successful in the business or legal worlds, in our experience if the partner of someone who is 'the concrete wall' decides at some point to leave the relationship it is generally a nightmare trying to negotiate sensible settlements about children and finance as there will be no shifting the inflexible partner in their view of what is fair. There is huge potential in this situation for separations or divorces to become overly complicated, destructive and hostile.

Mark is a barrister and seems to take delight in using skills better employed in the courtroom to ride roughshod over his wife, Jane, and adult daughter. When Jane inherited a small amount of money on the death of her mother she decided that she'd had enough of Mark's arrogance and bombastic behaviour and that she would leave him. Mark saw her decision as the first shot in a war of attrition and used every tactic to stall the divorce, argue over the joint assets and generally make Jane's life a living hell. This was despite the fact his solicitor had given him clear legal advice on what was a fair division of assets. Mark chose to ignore the advice as 'he knew best'. The outcome of his behaviour was that his wife (and daughter) decided to have no further dealings with him once they eventually divorced (the case having to go to court on numerous occasions because of Mark's inflexibility) and Mark has lost the opportunity to maintain a close relationship with his daughter and grandchildren.

The Playground Snitch?

This method of dealing with conflict can be summarised in the words, 'I'm telling on you!' It can be a form of emotional blackmail and is used to best effect when the couple has strong extended family, cultural or religious links where a partner can appeal to a 'higher authority' such as an older family member or religious leader to settle differences, which effectively takes the conflict out of the hands of the couple. This generally works if both parties are amenable to a third party settling disputes but, as every good mediator knows, solutions to disputes will usually fall apart if they have been imposed by an outsider rather than having been agreed between the couple. 'The playground snitch' can also wield power within a relationship if the other partner operates in the public arena in some way (say, a celebrity or a politician) or is dependent on a certain standing within a social setting. The threat of 'going public' with disputes can be an effective method of getting our own way whatever the rights and wrongs of the argument. The threat 'Do your worst' comes to mind when dealing with 'the playground snitch'.

Tim is the captain of the golf club, a magistrate and a prominent businessman in his local area. His partner, Sally, is well known within their social group for being very vocal publicly about her view of Tim's shortcomings, particularly when she has too much to drink. For the most part Sally's criticism is seen as trivial compared to the active part Tim plays in the community and not much notice is taken of it. Tim, however, tends to tiptoe around Sally and is very careful not to upset her for fear that she will compromise his standing in the local area. It does mean that Sally gets away with behaviour that would not be tolerated by someone with less of a public persona.

The Sulker?

Silence used as an act of aggression is a very common tactic in avoiding and dealing with conflict. It's difficult to have an argument with someone who quietly seethes, sometimes for days on end, and who resists all attempts to resolve disagreements with an open conversation. Usually 'the sulker' sees themselves as the aggrieved party – it's the 'you've hurt my feelings but I am not going to tell you how' approach to conflict. There is something very juvenile about 'the sulker' and in our experience they are probably best treated like a child who needs to be told very firmly at the start of a committed relationship that this behaviour will not be accepted.

Kevin has been with Marsha for eight years. They have no children, although they have tried IVF a few times. Kevin has to travel a lot in the UK for his job for a large supermarket chain. Marsha works part time as a librarian and is very resentful when Kevin has to go away. Kevin has noticed there is a distinct cooling in Marsha's mood towards him in the days before he goes away and when he comes back she is cold and distant for at least two to three days afterwards. Kevin feels aggrieved because Marsha knew that travelling for his job would be part of their life when they got together. He has tried to talk to Marsha about her sulking and silences but she denies that she is doing anything wrong. Kevin is seriously considering leaving the relationship.

The Saboteur?

On the face of it 'the saboteur' will look like 'the ostrich', falling passively into line at the first sign of conflict, but subtly they will do their hardest to undermine whatever has been agreed.

Julie wants to move home. Tariq, her partner, does not. On the face of it Tariq is happy to look at any number of houses with Julie but Tariq says they are either too big, too small, great location but awful house, great house but awful location, no south-facing garden, too close to their relatives, too far away from work. His list, of what he says are reasonable objections, is endless. While maintaining a passive façade, 'the saboteur' is an effective manipulator, but like 'the marytr' is difficult to pin down.

The Psycho?

It is not acceptable to feel that any conflict could provoke the total destruction of our relationship, no matter how long we have been in that relationship. If our partner makes it clear, overtly or implicitly, that any criticism or attempt to resolve things we are unhappy about, no matter how minor, will result in a cataclysmic overreaction by them then we are being controlled within that relationship. Put simply, it is unhealthy and abnormal and might possibly indicate our partner is emotionally unstable or, worse, has some sort of personality disorder.

You fear that any fight could be your last. Normal couples argue to resolve issues, but psychopaths make it clear that negative conversations will jeopardise the relationship, especially ones regarding their behaviour. Any of your attempts to improve communication will typically result

in the silent treatment. You apologise and forgive quickly, otherwise you know they will lose interest in you.
— *Psychopath free*, Jackson MacKenzie

Guidance
To summarise: conflict is not necessarily a bad thing!
But you must think carefully about your style (and the style of your partner) of resolving disagreement within your relationship. It's the 'how' you resolve issues, not necessarily the 'what' you argue about, that will be the best indicator of whether the relationship is built to last.

When thinking about conflict within your relationship, consider the following questionnaire. As always, answer the questions honestly with as much self-awareness as possible and remember there are no right or wrong answers.

1. Do you feel safe to express anger within your relationship?
2. If not, why not? What do you think will be the consequences of expressing anger?
3. What behaviour by your partner would be a 'deal-breaker' to you? Have you discussed with your partner what behaviour you would consider a major threat to the continuation of your relationship?
4. What was your experience of conflict in your childhood? Has this experience influenced how you express or deal with anger in your relationship?

5. How do you express your anger towards your partner? Are you able to articulate your anger in a controlled manner or do you use criticism, bullying or belittling words or verbal aggression under the guise of teasing?

6. How does your partner express their anger towards you?

7. What is your style of dealing with conflict within your relationship? Do you overreact as a matter of course, do you avoid conflict at all costs, do you placate, do you meet conflict head on, do you sulk or maintain silences for long periods or do you physically leave, are you inflexible in your approach or do you regularly appeal to a third party to adjudicate any disputes between you?

8. Do you or your partner use illness or other present or past difficulties as a method of avoiding criticism or conflict?

9. How does your partner deal with conflict within the relationship?

10. Do you continue to feel resentment/bitterness after an argument?

11. Do you feel guilty and in the wrong after an argument, no matter what the rights and wrongs of the argument may have been?

12. Are there 'no-go areas' in your relationship where certain topics cannot be discussed or cannot be discussed without a rapid or out-of-control escalation of the argument? Why are there no-go areas?

13. Do you feel that you have to tolerate your partner's anger or behaviour because you are more emotionally or financially dependent on your partner than they are on you?

14. Do you feel that you have to tolerate your partner's anger or behaviour because of external pressures on you, e.g. cultural, family or religious expectations?

Having identified how you deal with or avoid conflict in your relationship, what can you do to change the dynamic or resolve conflict in a way that it energises the relationship rather than destroys it?

There will be a difference in our approach if we are in longer-standing relationships than if we are just starting off. The newer the relationship the more we should be able to deal with conflict in a more positive fashion and can consciously try not to drop into destructive patterns. The longer the relationship the more entrenched we will be in how we relate to each other; the list of our grievances tends to be much, much more extensive and our tolerance of bad behaviour probably much shorter.

Whatever the length of your relationship, if conflict is threatening its stability then consider the following options:

1. Try to adopt the 'third position' during or, if that is not possible, after any arguments. This means that you able to stand back from your emotional response, examine the causes of any conflict and recognise the part you played in that dispute. We found that someone saying a simple but heartfelt 'Sorry' could

have profound effects on the continuing quality of the relationship.

2. If you are safely able to discuss issues that are contentious with your partner but children or others are usually around then arrange a day/evening away to talk to your partner in a calm environment. It might help if you write down the issues you see as generating conflict. It is important that this list does not become a catalogue of petty misdemeanours and gripes. You may find a game called *The Art of Couples' Conversation* (taoc.com) could help to initiate difficult conversations.

3. If it does not feel safe to express your anger or concerns to your partner then couple counselling may provide neutral territory to deal with conflict. Or if you are religious then your place of worship may well be able to offer guidance or counselling.

4. If your partner will not engage in any joint effort to change the way you deal with disputes and the level of conflict is affecting your mental or physical well-being then you may consider individual counselling for yourself. This can be accessed privately or through your GP. Be under no illusions. Counselling will not change your partner but it can help you change your own response to your situation.

And finally, although we are convinced 'how' we deal with conflict rather than 'what' we argue about will be one of the best indicators of whether the relationship will succeed or fail, when we were in practice we did see a number of common pitfalls (the what rather than the how) that led to unhappiness and the breakdown of relationships.

1. The trek to the countryside 'for the sake of the children'

Couples working and living in a city or large town suddenly become obsessed with the idea that their children need more green space, better schools and a larger house, and that can only be obtained by moving out of the city or town so that both or one of the couple needs to commute daily for long distances and for long hours. Usually one parent decides to stay at home or work locally, leaving the other to do the commuting. If money is no object, a city flat is purchased so that the commute is cut down to a few days a week and the likelihood of an affair grows. Commuting long distances is, at the very least, soul-destroying and boring and takes precious time away from our families.

Children very rarely develop emotional problems or are deeply unhappy because they live in a small house in a town or city. But children will be very unhappy indeed if their parents are unhappy, no matter how large the home or big the garden. In our opinion it is the quality of the parental relationship that in the main influences how well adjusted children become, not the quality or quantity of the bricks, mortar or greenery surrounding them.

2. Extensive international travelling for work or living abroad away from the relationship

Extensive international travel or living abroad apart for long periods of time rarely makes for a satisfactory relationship. Relationships need to be nurtured and that usually means spending regular time together, particularly if you have children together. Someone at some point will become bored and lonely during the time apart and the danger is that another person will be there able and willing to fill the void. It sounds fairly glamourous to be a tax exile (and there are more than you would think) where one or other of the couple can only be in the home country for a small proportion of the year, but again, in our experience, unless the couple is spending large amounts of time together it is inevitable the relationship will break down. Wealth opens up lots of opportunities in life and that includes more opportunities for affairs.

3. Treating the relationship as a business deal
Marrying just for tax or other financial reasons, treating a partner as a financial 'workhorse' or tolerating abusive or contemptuous treatment from a partner because of purely financial considerations are just some of the ways we can drop into accepting that the relationship is there purely to satisfy our material concerns. In our experience, a lack of a real emotional connection within a relationship will inevitably lead to the breakdown of the relationship at some point – at some level even the wealthiest oligarch needs to feel valued outside the depth of his or her wallet!

Most of us would like to think that we are accepted for exactly who we are within a close and loving relationship. The wives of multimillionaire New York bankers may feel happy that they receive a 'wives' bonus' for getting their children into the right schools, keeping attractive and thin and helping their husbands to entertain clients at all the smartest places, but in the end we are sure that it is deeply unsatisfying to be treated as an accessory to the career and ambition of another, even if that other is your long-term partner, civil partner or spouse, and no matter what the financial rewards might be.

Ask yourself: am I tied into my relationship purely because of financial considerations? If the answer is yes and I am not happy then how can I break/change my financial dependence? This might be best discussed with a legal or financial advisor.

It would be marvellous to think that we could live our lives, in theory anyway, without a disagreement, a quarrel or upset with our loved ones, but as this notion is totally unrealistic we must always be aware of the potential for conflict and be self-aware about how we deal with that conflict if our relationships are to have a chance to survive in a healthy state. How sad will it be to get to the end of our life and feel that we have wasted opportunities to live our emotional life free of regret or bitterness?

Guidance
Accept healthy conflict. Deal immediately with conflict. Once resolved, forget the conflict.

Remember:
> 'Bitterness is like cancer. It eats upon the host.'
> —Maya Angelou

Chapter Five
The 'other family' and the 'other friends'

'Every family has its own legend, morality and style,
and each child in that family interprets the legend,
morality and style in his or her own way.'
— **Dorothy Rowe**, *My Dearest Enemy,*
My Dangerous Friend:
Making and Breaking Sibling Bonds

Our own family life can be complicated and fraught with emotional minefields for the unwary. Usually, we have lived with our family at close quarters for many years and for good or bad we know the family rules, expectations and eccentricities. We know the 'light-the-blue-touch paper' moments of our family life, we know its legends, morality and style, and we deal with our family in a variety of ways based on our intimate knowledge of its inner workings.

But when we commit ourselves to a long-term relationship we step, almost blindfolded, into our partner's family territory, which can be akin to exploring an alien landscape without a map. When we fall in love we fall in love with that one special person but what most of us forget or just don't realise is that standing in the shadows close behind our beloved is a whole host of other individuals – parents, sisters, brothers, aunts, uncles and grandparents – together with that family's history, expectations, traditions, cultural and religious dictates and eccentricities. And this is without the possible hideous complications of children from previous relationships, ex-partners, ex-wives, ex-husbands or indeed the 'ex-others' families'.

If we are going to make our future with our partner, have children or entwine ourselves emotionally and financially with them then the 'other family' will be part of our lives for a very long time, whether we like it or not.

If we are very lucky our partner's family can accept us for who we are and welcome us wholeheartedly into their homes and hearts, but we lost count of how many relationships were damaged or even destroyed by the dislike, interference or downright malevolence of the 'other family' members.

Case Study

Jenna is an only child whose beloved parents were killed in a car crash when she was nineteen. Her aunt provided a home for her during university holidays but Jenna always felt that she was a nuisance to her aunt and was given a home by her under sufferance. She was twenty-six when she met Frank, a fellow civil servant. Frank is one of five siblings and is of West African descent. She was instantly warmly welcomed into his family by Frank's parents and siblings. Jenna felt that a door into another world had opened for her. 'My world went from monochrome into Technicolor and I will be forever grateful to Frank's family for the love and acceptance they have shown me,' she says.

***

In the West we are not too keen on the idea of arranged marriages, where the concerns and requirements of the family outweigh the wishes and desires of the individual child when choosing a partner, but when talking, not so many years ago, to the wives of judges in Pakistan they all said they were very happy in their marriages and had had implicit trust in their family to choose a 'good man', which presumably also meant 'from a good family'. This will raise the heckles of us women in the West but if such a family is considering prospective partners for their child they will make enquiries about background and family history to assess a new partner's suitability. This system of matchmaking, of course, has its own flaws and pitfalls and will not necessarily guarantee the success of a relationship, but it does mean that it is less likely there will be any shocks or surprises once a participant is inducted into the ways of the 'other family'.

In the West we tend to take a more individualistic approach to love. We make up our own minds about with whom we wish to spend our future life but this does mean that we can meet and fall in love with someone with no knowledge of their personal history or their present or past family circumstances. This is particularly true if we have met our partner in the cold, impersonal world of cyberspace. Before the advent of the internet the opportunities to meet someone generally came down to knowing someone through our local area, school, college or work, where we would probably know something of our partner's background. The internet offers anyone the opportunity to reinvent themselves or their background, which makes it much harder to unpick the truth before we move into a close relationship. There are regular jaw-dropping newspaper accounts by wives and husbands duped into bigamous marriages or partners manipulated into handing over fortunes to bogus lovers, with the fraudster only unmasked by an unguarded Facebook picture or posting.

Guidance

It is unwise to view our partner in isolation from their family and background.

If at all possible, we should meet the 'other family' and see how we are treated by them before we commit to a long-term relationship because, wherever or however we have met our partner, it can be a nasty shock to realise that although we have found our soulmate, their family, for any number of reasons, does not share the same view.

'*Stephen's mother once said to me, "We don't like you because you don't fit into our family." On another occasion she learned by chance that the Hawkings were planning to move to Cambridge so that they could be there when the marriage foundered, as they were sure it eventually would.*' Interview by Joanna Moorhead of Jane Hawking (*Guardian*, 16 May 2015)

Jokes about interfering dragons of mothers-in-law were the staple diet of old-style comedians but it is no joke if we feel belittled or devalued by our partner's family.

Case Study

Dylan is a twenty-five-year-old painter and decorator. He left school at sixteen, is hard-working, self-employed and is making a success of his business. He adores his girlfriend, Louisa, who is a beautician. Dylan has asked Louisa to move in with him. Louisa's father, Joe, does not like Dylan, although does not seem able to say precisely why this is so. He calls Dylan 'I.B.' short for 'Idiot Boy'. Dylan feels Louisa should stop her father from belittling him but Louisa adores Joe and is reluctant to talk to her father about Dylan's concerns. Dylan can see that Joe is anxious that Dylan is replacing him as the central man in Louisa's life but finds Joe's constant rudeness towards him very upsetting. Louisa finds that she is stuck in the middle of the two men.

***

We saw time and time again that differences in family backgrounds or how a family treated a newcomer into the family could cause huge problems for couples even though the individuals in the relationship were well suited. It was as if one or other of the families cast a large and dark shadow over the relationship, which took a lot of emotional maturity and understanding by the couple to handle and overcome if the relationship was going to survive long term.

It seemed to us that a relationship breakdown could be precipitated by certain fundamental differences in a couple's family backgrounds, particularly those concerning religion, culture, education, social class and wealth.

Religion

If we have been brought up in a family with strong religious views it may be very difficult to be able to choose a partner from another faith or who has no particular faith. It takes a strong-minded person to be able to override such a fundamental element of our upbringing and live our lives as we wish, rather than how our faith dictates. It could mean rejecting not only our faith but being rejected by our own family and wider community, and this is a daunting prospect for many of us.

In extreme cases the 'family juggernaut' can threaten to squash any attempt at inter-faith relationships by any means possible: so-called 'honour killings' are the response of a family to an individual member of that family having a relationship out of their faith and community. Leaving aside such extreme methods, if we are not accepted by our partner's family, for whatever reason, our partner may be put under severe emotional/economic pressure to fall in line with the family's wishes and may have no alternative but to abandon the relationship.

Case Study

Ben and his girlfriend, Julia, have been together for three years and are in their early thirties. They do not live together and Ben still lives in the family home. Ben is Jewish. Julia is not and has no particular faith. Ben and Julia are both highly educated and met while working as lawyers at a large London law firm. They share a love of opera, theatre and walking and generally get on very well together. Julia, however, has never met Ben's family. Ben knows that his family, particularly his father, would have a fit if they knew he was with someone that was not Jewish. His parents constantly produce suitable Jewish girls for him to take out and Ben's excuses about why he does not want to meet up with them are wearing thin. Ben jokes that his father would rather he was in a gay relationship with a Jewish man than be married to a non-Jewish woman. The Jewish faith passes down the female line so unless Julia is prepared to convert to Judaism any children she has with Ben would not be Jewish. Julia is conscious that if she wants children with Ben then he has to confront his family and tell them about her. It remains to be seen whether Ben's loyalty to his family and faith is greater than for his love for Julia.

Case Study

Laura met Anand, who is from a traditional Sikh family, at their large West London comprehensive. They began to go out together in their sixth form, although Anand always told his parents and siblings that Laura was just part of a large group of friends at school. Anand knows that his parents will expect him to eventually marry a girl from his community. Laura and Anand chose to study at the same university and now in their third year they live together in shared accommodation.

Unfortunately for the couple, Anand's parents decided to visit him without telling him of their plans. When they arrived at the student house it was obvious that he was living in the same room as Laura and a terrible argument ensued. Anand stood firm and told his parents that he had no intention of breaking up with Laura. His parents said they would not speak to him again unless he broke off the relationship and they immediately stopped a monthly allowance they were making to him. Anand has been inundated with texts, emails and calls from his siblings, pleading with him to end his relationship with Laura and make his peace with his parents. Although Anand has told Laura that he will not bow to family pressure, Laura is mature enough to realise that he will never be truly happy if he is permanently estranged from his family. With great sadness Laura is considering ending the relationship once they graduate.

Culture

With greater international travel for pleasure and business it is far more likely in the twenty-first century than in previous times for couples from different countries and societies to meet and start relationships. Cultural differences can certainly add flavour and excitement to a relationship, but as one partner of an international marriage said, 'At some point it's likely someone wants to go home.'

If you are beginning a relationship with someone from another country ask yourself this: 'Would I be prepared to live away from my country of birth for ever?' If the answer is no then you may well be storing up trouble for a later date. It is of particular importance if you are thinking of having children. If you are in a long-term relationship that fails and your partner wants to move to back to Doncaster from London with your children it's one thing, but if they want to go home to New Zealand with them it's another.

Case Study

Jamie is from London and is in his forties. He has been married to Maria for four years. They met when Jamie was on a business trip to Brazil, had a whirlwind romance and married after two months together. Maria has never liked living in England. She has found making English friends difficult and finds the weather a particular challenge. Over the years she has become more and more depressed and has begged Jamie to find work in Brazil, which he says is impossible. This is causing arguments, which in turn is making Maria more miserable. It's easy for Jamie to see that in hindsight Maria should have come to England before they married to see if she could set up home here permanently.

Cultural attitudes and differences can also become very apparent if we have children.

Case Study

Khow is from a Chinese background and was brought up in Liverpool. He has been with Kay, who is from Lancashire, for twenty years and they have two children. Kay has always been warmly accepted into Khow's family and she gets on well with his parents and siblings, but Kay admits that she was taken aback by Khow's attitude to parenting once the children were born – it seemed very strict and not as loving as she had expected. Khow's mother explained to her that culturally they expected the children to be given strict boundaries, and expectations of their behaviour were very high. The Western view that children should be given freedom and independence with a more relaxed relationship with their parents did not sit well within a Chinese household. Kay listened to Khow's mother and realised that Khow's idea of protecting and loving his children, although different from hers, was nonetheless as valid. Together Kay and Khow have brought up two bright and well-adjusted children.

***

Families have their own peculiar traditions and customs, which newcomers can find exciting or bewildering in the initial stages of a relationship, or downright irritating after years together. Hearty, sports-mad families cannot quite understand the non-sporty book-lover, families with a love of practical jokes and aggressive teasing find the tears of a shocked new partner genuinely perplexing, teetotal families will view the pub-loving pint drinker's behaviour shocking, and so it goes on. One particular custom that seems to cause arguments is one partner's insistence that every Sunday be spent with their family. We would all like to think lunches en famille would follow the Hollywood picture of Italian or French family meals, where delicious food is consumed on a sun-dappled terrace as laughter and chatter swirls around the table. Sunday lunch at the in-laws' is not necessarily a British custom but it was mentioned to us more than once as the cause of weekly tension. The children are bored, conversation is stilted or centres on the same topics every week, and the feeling that another day has slipped away rather than enjoyed precedes the inevitable squabble on the way home.

Guidance
Flexibility is the key word here.
Insisting on your partner adhering to particular customs of your own family may not make for happy family gatherings.

Allowing your partner to negotiate their own relationship with your family will make for happier relations all around.

***

Education

Certain families are highly vocal about their own intellectual superiority.

There is something very belittling and demeaning to become part of another family who by words or deeds makes us feel that our opinions, views or our very being is worthless.

Case Study

John has been married to Libby for twenty-five years. Libby is from a family who for generations not only all went to Cambridge but to a particular college at Cambridge. John went to university in the Midlands and became a highly successful and well-paid accountant in a large international company. Over the years Libby's family has made it clear to John that his opinions on most topics are not valued and the fact that neither of his two children with Libby went to Cambridge was, as Libby's father put it, 'because of the watering down of the gene pool by you, John'.

Libby is very apologetic about her family and thankfully John is secure enough in his own success that he now finds such insults amusing. John agreed with Libby many years ago that he would limit his appearance at family events, usually using work as an excuse. By limiting the time John spends with Libby's family the couple have managed to override her family's disapproval of John.

Social class

In the past the class system in Britain was presented as a simple model of working, middle and upper classes, with few relationships crossing the social divides. Nowadays, it seems ridiculous to think that differences in social class of our families could play any part in affecting our choice of partner or contribute to problems within our relationships, and even the British royal family has had to accept non-royals (the Duchess of Cambridge being a prime example) into the family – unthinkable in previous generations. But in Britain and many countries around the world there is still a social elite that has a particular style of living and has wide social networks primarily based on family history and connections, education and wealth.

Case Study

Moira is attractive, well-educated and good fun. She met George when they were working as economists at a well-known bank. Moira was brought up with her much-loved siblings by Josie, their single parent mother, on a council estate in Sussex. Josie always impressed on her children the value of a good education and all the children are bright and ambitious, going to college or university and securing high-earning careers. George was brought up on a large country estate in Hampshire that had been his grandparents' home, is the younger of two brothers and was brought up with a good deal of material comfort. His father is a barrister and his mother a solicitor. George and Moira got on well together, both are ambitious and doing well in their careers, and Moira had expected to be welcomed as a matter of course by George's family.

Not so. At their first meeting at a restaurant his parents were friendly but guarded, and in not so many words made it clear to Moira that they felt George should be with someone of his own background and social standing.

Moira felt 'a nobody'. It did not matter to George's family who she was but it did matter to whom she was connected, and a mother still living on a council estate would simply not do. George and Moira split up after George seemed to cool towards their relationship soon after Moira's meeting with his parents. His loyalty to his family outweighed his feelings for Moira. Moira feels she had a lucky escape and that if the relationship had gone any further she would have constantly been under pressure to be something she was not.

***

Family money
Some of the most difficult divorce cases involve family trusts and inherited money. There's an old Lancashire saying, 'There's nobbut three generations between a clog and a clog.' Which roughly translates as 'One generation to make the money. One generation to live on the money. And one generation to lose the money!' Families with inherited wealth rarely like giving up any amount to an outsider, no matter how long that person may have been married or has been in a relationship with a family member who benefits from that inherited wealth. If you are in a long-term relationship with someone whose income and capital is based on family money you will be inextricably tied into

their family, and woe betide you if you do not toe the family line or, worse still, leave the relationship with expectations of taking any of the family money with you.

Case Study

Penny met Simon when she worked for his father as his PA at the large family-owned engineering firm in the East Midlands. The firm had been set up by Simon's great-grandfather and Simon is a beneficiary of a family trust. Although Simon is a director of the company, his main income and capital was channelled through the family trust. Penny and Simon have been married for fifteen years and have three children, all at private schools paid for by the trust. At Simon's behest Penny gave up work when their first child was born and by her own admittance they have lived extremely comfortably, with capital being advanced to Simon by the trust to buy their home, expensive cars and fund holidays, etc.

Penny recently found out that Simon has been having an affair with her best friend for a number of years. She was devastated and decided that the marriage was at an end. She has been shocked to find that the family trust owns the family home and the trustees have told Penny that they will not be advancing Simon any further money for school fees or to fund her and the children's monthly expenditure until the divorce proceedings are resolved. Simon's actual salary is minuscule compared to the family money he has enjoyed. Simon now says that Penny and the children will have to live in much-reduced circumstances and the children will have to leave private schooling as he cannot afford to pay for it. The divorce is gearing up to be a highly contentious battle.

****

We tend to shy away from talking about money with our partners in the early stages of a relationship and discussions of hard, cold facts about money do not sit well with the idea of love and romance.

We will deal with the issue of money and who holds the purse strings in relationships in a later chapter, but we cannot stress how vitally important it is that where the 'other family' holds the family purse strings you must have a very clear idea about how this may impact on your long-term relationship, your future financial security and that of any children you may have together. It would be wise to obtain legal advice before you marry, begin long-term cohabitation or have children with someone who benefits from family money.

So, how do we deal with our loved one's family when either we do not like them or they us? If you are in the early stages of your relationship ask yourself:

1. Have I met my partner's family? How welcoming have they been to me? Have any problems been raised by my partner's family about our relationship?

2. How realistic are my expectations of my partner's long-term loyalty to me over their loyalty to their own family if they do not accept me? How important is it to my partner that regular and close contact is maintained with their family? It may well be that my partner does not have a close emotional or geographic closeness to their family and so their disapproval has no real impact on our relationship.

3. Are any fundamental religious, political, cultural educational or class differences between us? Would the family be prepared to accept me, say, if I changed religion?

4. If my partner is from a different country to me, how realistic, long term, is our relationship? Would I be prepared to live in my partner's home country for ever?

5. Would my partner's family be able to interfere substantially in any of our financial arrangements?

6. Would I be prepared to distance myself or cut myself off from my own religion, culture or family to maintain my relationship? Would this cause considerable anguish to my own family?

7. Am I asking my partner to distance themselves or cut themselves off from their own religion, culture or family to maintain our relationship? In the long run, will my partner be happy with such an estrangement?

If we are already in a long-term relationship where substantial problems between us and our partner are being caused by outside family interference then it will be much more difficult to change a destructive family dynamic but, take heart, it is not impossible.

1. As with any conflict, we should try to take the 'third person' approach. We may well have felt belittled, undervalued or treated downright badly by the 'other family' (or at least one or two key people within it) and over the years this will have built up huge resentment and anger, but can we step back and look at the situation less emotionally? Can we think about where we stand in

any family tension and are we able to do anything about it? Would it be possible to sit down with members of the family and discuss any problems or issues?

2. Are we able to agree a compromise with our partner to limit the time we have to spend with their family?

3. Can we respect the fact that our partner should spend time with their family without compromising their loyalty to us?

4. If we or our partner are not able to resolve our differences about family interference, divided loyalties or mutual dislike then we should consider couple counselling. As with any conflict, it is not really to do with what we are arguing about but how we argue about it, and this relates just as much to issues relating to the 'other family' as to anything else.

And as a final thought, we should not underestimate the anguish that can be caused by new partners coming into a family dynamic, not only for the new partner but also the 'other family'. Professor Tanya Byron, a psychologist, writing in *The Times* (16 February 2015), responded to her correspondent 'Felicity', who had written to her in a state of distress for advice because her son's new wife wished him to cut all ties with his previously close-knit family.

'Given that your son is a man you love and respect, I am interested why he would love a woman that his family clearly struggle to like. I suspect that he must feel very torn in all this but fundamentally and quite appropriately loyal to the woman he is married to. The heartbreak for all must be huge.'

The 'other family' may seem an irrelevance to us in the first flush of romance and love, but the reality is that unless we are very lucky this family will most certainly have a profound influence on not only the long-term success or failure of our relationship but our very happiness. The old adage 'Check the stable before you buy the horse' may be an old-fashioned and crude entreaty to would-be lovers but it is an unwise person who fails to at least peep at the 'other family' before we jump head first into a full-blown relationship.

***

Friends – the company we choose
It would be very wise to have a peep at our partner's circle of friends.

There's an old song that goes:

> 'Twas an evening in October
> I'll confess I wasn't sober,
> I was carting home a load with manly pride
> When my feet began to stutter
> And I fell in the gutter
> And a pig came up and lay down by my side
> Till a lady, passing by, did chance to say
> 'You can tell a man who boozes
> By the company he chooses'
> Then the pig got up and slowly walked away.
> —*The Famous Pig Song* (traditional folk song)

We'd say that it is true you can tell a lot about a potential partner by looking at the company they choose; their circle of friends will give us an indication of our partner's general view of life – for good or bad. This is particularly relevant if you have met your partner away from any social context, say via the internet, where you have not had an opportunity to see them with family, friends or work colleagues. If our partner seems to be surrounded by drug users, heavy drinkers, gamblers or criminals, what does that say about them? Conversely, if our partner has very few or no friends, shouldn't we be asking ourselves why not? Is it because our partner is difficult or socially inept or charmless or does not see the value in friendship?

Case Study

Sheena met Gary in a pub. She was celebrating a friend's birthday and he was celebrating with his teammates and friends after winning a rugby match. Gary had responded to a dare given by one of his mates to kiss the first girl who walked by. Sheena liked the kiss and their relationship has blossomed. But while Sheena has found that Gary is kind, generous and fun to be with, when he gets together with his friends he is a different person.

'I hate Gary when he is around his mates. They drink way too much, are loud and, frankly, a bit scary en masse. There is a "mate's code" which I think is very sexist, particularly the "what happens on tour stays on tour" attitude to wives and partners. I don't want to be the whiny girlfriend but I cannot stand the way they become some sort of schoolboy mob when they are out.' Gary's whole social life revolves around the rugby club and he is loyal to the group, who he has known for years. It's doubtful whether he will sacrifice this loyalty for a new girlfriend.

****

If our partner is part of a well-established friendship group it is more than likely they will have some influence on whether the relationship will flourish, dependent on whether or not the group is prepared to accept you willingly into their fold.

Case Study

Tilly met Sean through a speed-dating evening. Their romance took off very quickly and, while initially they were more than happy to spend all their free time together, after a few months Sean was keen to introduce Tilly to his close-knit circle of friends from schooldays. Sean organised a meal at a local restaurant for them to meet. 'It was a disaster,' says Tilly. 'Sean has eight friends he has known since school – male and female. From the minute I met them they made it clear I was some kind of interloper and spent the whole evening talking about the "good old days". One friend, Anna, was particularly keen to claim ownership of Sean, draping herself around him, laughing hysterically at his jokes and interrupting every conversation I tried to initiate with, "Do you remember when…?" I found out later that Sean and her had been an item on and off for years.'

Tilly felt that the only way they could move forward with their relationship would be if she had very limited contact with the friends but when she told Sean this, he became very upset and told her that he could not contemplate his partner not becoming part of his friendship set. This prompted the first big argument of the relationship and the jury is out on whether Sean and Tilly can negotiate a compromise. Tilly thinks that Sean is being unrealistic as she feels most friendship groups evolve and change over the years anyway, and that he is being very immature to put loyalty to this group over the potential of a long-term committed partnership. But Sean sees the group as fundamental to his life and would feel bereft if they were not part of his life. Tilly is going to have an uphill struggle if she thinks she will be able to wrest Sean away from this group. Eventually, she might be asking herself if it is worth the trouble.

Ask yourself:

1. Does my partner have an established group of friends?
2. On the whole, have they been welcoming to me?
3. If not, why not?
4. Am I expecting my new partner to place their loyalty to me over their friends?
5. Is it realistic to expect my partner to place my needs and wishes over those of their group of friends?
6. What kind of friends is my partner associated with?
7. Do I have any concerns about my partner's friends and the influence they have on my partner?
8. Does my partner have no (or few) friends?
9. Is there explanation for why my partner has no (or few) friends?
10. Do I have an established group of friends?
11. Do my friends (on the whole) like my partner?

12. If not, why not?

13. Do I trust the judgement of my friends?

14. Do I believe that my friends have my best interests at heart if they express their concerns about my partner to me?

15. Has my partner attempted to isolate me from my friendship group? Please see Chapter Nine for more detail on this point.

Disliking our partner's family and/or friends is not necessarily a deal-breaker. After all, we will say, if we are in love and fully committed to a long-term relationship, why should outside influences really matter? But once the 'love drug' phase has begun to wear off it is important that we see our partner in a realistic light and in the context of their other relationships. If we are unable to see how our partner fits into the wider picture of their family or friends, how can we gain a better understanding of them?

Chapter Six
Sex

'Sex makes fools of us all.'
—**Anonymous**

Every individual, every culture, every religious group and every generation has a view about sex – the when, where, how and who does what to whom. We are bombarded on a daily basis by books, newspapers and magazine articles, plays or films, all bursting with advice on how to deal with the tricky issue of sexual relations in the twenty-first century. When we were researching material for this article we came across scores of articles about sex, these from mainstream national newspapers in the last six months alone:

'Share and share alike. Matt Rudd checks in at a hotel for swingers.'
'Sex, lies and the end of monogamy. The couple crisis.'
'Inside a Tinder marriage – there are three people in our relationship.'
'Every man I saw was a target. Meet the women addicted to sex.'
'Adultery: Can it actually help to save a marriage?'

Numerous websites, claiming millions of worldwide subscribers, exist for the sole purpose of creating opportunities for casual sexual 'hook-ups' and the phrases 'booty call' or 'friends with benefits' have reached common parlance. It no doubt piques our curiosity to hear and read about another's sex life, and if the media is to be believed a substantial proportion of the population is vigorously engaged in some sort of sexual subterfuge or dodgy sexual practices. And if this is your idea of a satisfactory lifestyle, this is not the chapter (or book) for you. We are interested in relationships that involve a committed, emotional connection between two people. We are not interested in polyamorous relationships or 'screw and leave' sexual gymnastics that involve the exchange of bodily fluids and nothing else.

****

It might sound naïve or downright boring but in our experience no matter how much experimentation we have dabbled in during our youth (or beyond), a substantial proportion of us, male and female, gay, bisexual, transgender or straight, at some point in our lives will want a lasting sexual relationship with one trusted partner, a partner with whom we feel safe and loved. And although the general message through the media is that sex is overwhelmingly the upmost important aspect of our relationships, we found that on many occasions conflict relating to money, lifestyle or children far outweighed sexual problems. Indeed, we found that relationships could last for many, many years with little or no sex and that the breaking point could be triggered by events or behaviour wholly unrelated to an unsatisfactory sex life.

Couples in new relationships might shudder at the thought that sex does not necessarily continue to carry the heightened sense of desire we usually feel at the beginning of our relationship, but the comfort of a shared history over many years, children, financial entanglements, family ties, companionship and any number of other factors can push sex down the list of important matters keeping us in our long-term relationship.

It is a fact that keeping sexual momentum going in a long-term relationship is much more difficult than searching a website for the nearest sex-without-strings liaison. David Aaronovitch, in his review (*The Times*, 4 April 2015) of *Sex by Numbers: What Statistics Can Tell Us About Sexual Behaviour* by David Spiegelhalter, writes:

Perhaps the most surprising revelation, however, is the most counter-intuitive. We live, after all, in a highly sexualised society, full of porn, naughty advertising and pre-watershed swearing. So we must be having more sex, right? Wrong. We're having a lot less. Median frequency of sex with an opposite sex partner in the previous four weeks among sixteen to forty-four-year-olds is down from five times in 1990 to three in 2010.

****

In Chapter One we gave the following advice:

'If at all possible it is wise to live full time with your partner for at least a year without making any major life decisions such as marrying, having a child or entwining your financial affairs.'

This one-year rule is also sensible when applied to our sexual compatibility as in the first flush of romance our sexual compatibility will generally be obscured by the 'love drug' phase of our relationship. The weight we place on the significance of sex within our relationship will vary from couple to couple and the expectations of sex will be unique to each couple so that it is only after the relationship has settled down that we can begin to discover whether we are truly sexually compatible – and this is only if we have been fortunate enough to be able to live with each other as even in the twenty-first century certain cultures, religious groups and families are firmly set against couples living together or having sex before marriage. Many of us worry whether we are 'normal' sexually but is there such a thing as 'normal'?

What might be normal for a couple in a BDSM relationship (where bondage, dominance, submission, sadism and masochism are practised) might be very abnormal for another. Some relationships thrive even though penetrative sex is not possible or a partner is impotent as long as other expressions of affection and intimacy are shown such as cuddling, hugging and kissing. In any intimate relationship we have to test what feels normal and right for us sexually without feeling coerced, bullied, belittled or pressured into sexual activity that feels dangerous (emotionally or physically) or shameful for us.

Case Study

Rob and Judy, in their early thirties, have lived together for eight months. At the beginning of their relationship Rob made it clear that he was sexually adventurous and had been part of a 'swingers' group that participated in group sex. Judy had been in several monogamous relationships but felt she was open to experimentation. After several weekends away with like-minded couples she feels that this lifestyle is not for her, particularly as she suffers intense pangs of jealousy when she sees Rob with another woman. Rob has no intention of becoming monogamous and although Judy feels that she and Rob are very compatible sexually when they are alone, she is on the point of leaving him as she realises Rob's expectations of the sexual side of their relationship will inevitably wear away her trust of and love for him. This has been a very difficult decision for Judy but at least she has the freedom to go without being bound by considerations about children or financial ties.

****

When considering the sexual side of our relationship, as with other aspects of it, we need to bear in mind our four main factors – realism, integrity, self-awareness and knowledge.

Realism
Research has shown that females and males do express their emotional and sexual needs differently.

'*Differences between the genders are significant and are one of the factors contributing to relational and psychosexual issues that can lead to considerable distress in adult life.*' Janice Hiller, '*Sex, Mind, and Emotion*' (This is an essay in a compilation – full title in bibliography.)

Women's sexual desire may be influenced to a greater

extent than men by their own body image, anxiety about family or work stresses. Under these circumstances sex can be seen as just another pressure or duty, especially if a partner is unable or unwilling to see the correlation between the external stress and a lack of responsiveness to sexual advances.

We may or may not have had sex before we fall in love but it's more than likely that after we have fallen in love we will automatically expect to have a blissful sex life with our beloved. But if we are in a new relationship it is unrealistic to suppose that because we have fallen in love we will be immediately sexually compatible. Chemistry, technique, timing and desire all go into the mix to produce a good sexual experience and just because it is less than satisfactory at the beginning it does not mean that it is doomed to failure. For those of us brought up watching romantic Hollywood movies or porn where effortless mind blowing orgasms are a given it can be difficult to accept that sex with our loved one can be anything but automatically wonderful.

Elisabeth Lloyd is a professor of biology at Indiana University with a specialist interest in sex:

"It is harder for women now than women in the 1970's," says Lloyd. "All that enlightening work has been lost. I get young college women now saying the same things to me every time, 'I don't know what's wrong with me', misinformed by what they see on screen. For 94 per cent of women what they see universally on screen is false, and that is kind of tragic." *The Times*, 1 March 2016

Case Study
Tony and Rosie are in their forties, both with a marriage

behind them and no children. They have known each other for ten years as colleagues. There has always been a mutual attraction between them and their friendship has gradually developed into a deep regard and affection. In due course they went on a number of dates and when they eventually found themselves in bed they expected 'fireworks'. In fact, it was more like a 'damp squib'! Probably, if they had been younger they would have felt embarrassed and awkward and would have avoided all future contact. Thankfully, Tony managed to make Rosie laugh by telling her 'practice makes perfect' and on their next attempt all went well and five years on they are still together and both feel they have a good sex life.

****

Guidance
Communication is key.
If your first sexual experiences together are not wholly satisfactory or desire has been reduced by external worries such as family, work or body image then talk to each other. There should be no place for embarrassment or awkwardness in a committed relationship. There are scores of books available, offering advice on sexual matters (probably even at your local library).

And if you want to be chilled by how a lack of communication about sexual matters can kill a relationship, read *On Chesil Beach* by Ian McEwan, a standard text for many aspiring couple counsellors.

It is also, in our view, unrealistic to expect to maintain

an all-consuming sex life in a long-term relationship. If you have been together for years and are as happy with your sex life together as you were when you first met then well done! The reality for a large majority of us is that sex settles into more of a statement about our intimacy and trust with each other rather than an expression of heightened desire and passion. And this only becomes a problem if one partner's expectations are different from the other's.

But don't despair! It is possible to maintain a good sex life in a long-term relationship. Emily Nagoski teaches women's sexuality at Smith College in the USA. In her book *Come as You Are: The Surprising New Science That Will Transform your Sex Life* she explains that research (the Gottmans again) has shown that maintaining a close, connected and trusting friendship with your partner and making sex a priority can help maintain a satisfying sex life in long-term relationships.

****

We say that maintaining a trusting friendship goes to the heart of the points we have made previously in this book. If you aren't kind to your partner, you don't appreciate or respect your partner and do not deal with conflict in a constructive manner, the reality is that it is more than likely your sex life will suffer and be non-existent or at best unsatisfactory. The fact is that what is going on outside the bedroom has a huge effect on what is going on inside it.

So, one way to maintain a good sex life in a long-term committed relationship is to make sure that we don't drop into negative habits of passive/aggressive behaviour, constant criticism or contemptuous behaviour towards our partner. The rewards for making a small amount of effort towards each other on a day-to-day basis can be translated into love in the bedroom; a win-win for us all!

Guidance

There is nothing like seething resentment or contempt within a relationship to kill off desire and passion in the bedroom.

Case Study

Peter and Tara have been together for twenty years and have two teenage children. Peter has a high libido and expects to have sex at least twice a day. In the early days of their relationship Tara's libido matched Peter's but over the years Tara has felt constantly criticised by Peter and she has suspected that he has been unfaithful to her on a number of occasions, which has upset her greatly. This has made Tara suspicious and resentful and she finds that her feelings have spilled over into reducing her sexual feeling towards Peter. Peter complains bitterly that his 'needs' are being ignored and has told Tara, 'If you won't have sex with me when I want it then I'll look elsewhere.' It is a vicious circle.

The more he threatens and Tara feels bullied the less she wants to have sex with him, but then the more Peter feels neglected and is critical.

****

Integrity and self-awareness

Our sexuality is at the heart of most adult committed relationships. And honesty and self-awareness about our sexual identity will be a major influence on the success of our relationships during our lives.

As we saw in Chapter Two, our family upbringing can influence our expectations of relationships and love. It can also heavily influence our expectations of sexual relationships. If we have been told by our family that sex is forbidden, dirty, shameful or sinful, it may be very difficult to overcome these messages to have a genuinely satisfying sex life unless we seek professional help. If we have been abused sexually during our childhood then it is likely that without professional help we will suffer sexual dysfunction or be prone to addictive sexual behaviour.

Research has also shown that coming from a difficult or fractured family can influence our sexual behaviour.

'Children who experience interpersonal relationships as undependable are less likely to expect commitment from a partner and are more likely to engage in unrestricted sexual behaviour, with weaker attachments.' Janice Hiller, *'Sex, Mind, and Emotion'*

Guidance
If you are experiencing difficulty in your sexual relationships (or lack of sexual relationships) because of the 'family whisper' of your childhood or because of continuing religious or cultural messages, please do not suffer in silence. Speak to your GP to access specialist help.

****

In David Spiegelhalter's book *Sex by Numbers: What Statistics Can Tell Us About Sexual Behaviour* he writes that it is likely around 1.2 million adults in the UK are gay/lesbian or bisexual. It is sometimes difficult to obtain precise figures as even with the loosening of attitudes to same-sex relationships, coming to terms with being gay or bisexual is difficult for many, especially in the light of religious, cultural or family objections, although in a recent survey a high percentage of eighteen to twenty-year-olds identified themselves as bisexual.

Professor Oliver Sacks, in his autobiography, *On The Move*, tells of a conversation with his parents in the early 1950s when he was a young man:

And then my father got on to what was really worrying him. 'You don't seem to have many girlfriends,' he said. 'Don't you like girls?'
'They're all right,' I answered, wishing the conversation would stop.
'Perhaps you prefer boys?' he persisted.
'Yes, I do – but it's just a feeling – I have never "done" anything,' and then I added fearfully, 'Don't tell Ma – she won't be able to take it.'
But my father did tell her, and the next morning she came down with a face of thunder, a face I had never seen before. 'You are an abomination,' she said. 'I wish you had never been born.'

It would be nice to think that such conversations were a museum piece, having no place in 2015 onwards, but, sadly, it is still the case that men and women are forced into marriage or heterosexual relationships because of the disapproval of their families or communities. It is a deep sadness for the individual to have to live a lie about such a fundamental part of their character but inevitably it will also be a great sadness and upset for the person living with them who is ignorant of their true sexual identity. The following case study does not describe an isolated incident.

Case Study

Maddy is in her twenties and from an evangelical Christian background. She met Sonny at their church three years ago and to the delight of their respective families they are engaged. Sonny is funny, charismatic, good looking and highly educated and Maddy could not believe her luck when he began to pay her attention. They spend most weekends at church activities and have done little more than hold hands and kiss. Sonny has told Maddy that there is no rush to marry and they both agree that they will not have sex until after marriage. Unbeknown to Maddy, his family or church friends, Sonny is gay and during the week plays an active part in a city gay bar scene. Sonny has no wish to upset his parents or community and sincerely believes that he will be able to compartmentalise the two strands of his life if eventually he is pressurised into marrying Maddy. Sonny does not mean to harm Maddy but his lack of honesty could have devastating consequences for her in later years.

****

Being honest about one's sexual preferences early on in our relationship can also save a lot of anguish later on. At least at the beginning of a relationship our partner has a better chance of making a decision about whether they are willing to participate in our fantasies without the complication of years of layers of deceit.

Case Study

Lorna has been married to Paul for fifteen years. She would say that they have a good sex life and are generally very happy together, running their successful printing business. One midweek day Paul told Lorna that he felt unwell and left the office to go home. Lorna rang Paul a few times on his mobile phone and when she did not get an answer left the office to go home too. When she got home Paul did not seem to be at home, although she called and called. Thinking that Paul had gone to the doctor, Lorna was just about to leave when she heard a faint noise from their bedroom.

Fearing that Paul had collapsed, Lorna charged upstairs and flung open the door, only to find there was no one in the room. Puzzled, she called out Paul's name again, to be answered by a shamefaced Paul coming out of their en suite bathroom dressed head to toe in her clothes and fully made up. Paul confessed that secretly he had been dressing in her clothes for years. He was not gay but had identified himself as a transvestite years before, something he had neglected to share with Lorna.

After the initial shock Lorna was able to talk to Paul openly about his need to dress as a woman and once she realised that he is not attracted to other men she has been supportive ever since. Her one rule is that Paul does not go out publicly in women's clothes, although this is something he would like to do. Lorna feels that although Paul has not been as honest as he could have been with her over the years of the marriage she says, 'It is not like he has had an affair or has a secret family somewhere. And, anyway, he is still the gorgeous Paul I have loved for over fifteen years.'

****

Guidance
It is essential we try to be as honest as possible about our sexual orientation or preferences before we commit to long-term relationships and particularly before we have children.

Although we realise that some research shows that our sexual identity may be fluid and change over the years, in our experience most individuals who suddenly leave long-established heterosexual relationships to begin a relationship with a same-sex partner have known of (or suspected) their true sexual orientation from a young age. It is not uncommon for a rejected partner or child to suffer severe emotional problems and if you have been left by a partner in these circumstances and feel unable to accept his/her decision, it is vital to access professional help or at least find a support group.

It is not acceptable to be bullied, coerced or dragged into sexual acts with our partner that in the long run leave us feeling embarrassed or ashamed or that endanger our health. A loving partner who we can trust will either not ask us to participate in such behaviour or will accept our refusal. If they do not, then have a long, hard think about where the relationship is headed.

Judy, in our case study above, was not prepared to enter into a permanent 'swinging' lifestyle and left the relationship. This may be more difficult if you have children, a complicated family or financial history together, but continually feeling that you are being asked to participate in sexual acts that go to the very soul of your well-being seems to us to be a particularly pernicious form of abuse. We liked the story of a wife of many years standing who was asked by her husband to agree to anal sex as 'everyone else was doing it'. Her reply made us laugh. 'Sure. As long as you try it first.'

With the advent of the internet the opportunities for humiliating an ex-partner have grown. There have been many reported cases of 'revenge porn', where a partner has consented to being filmed having sex, that has then been posted online for the world to see after the relationship has ended, with the victim feeling so humiliated that they have become severely depressed and/or suicidal. In certain circumstances in England and Wales it is a criminal act to share private, sexual photographs or films that have been made for private use. Unless you know you would be able to cope with intimate details of your body/sex life being made public, do not consent to be filmed or be photographed by a partner, no matter how flattered you are or what assurances you are given that the images will never be made public.

****

Guidance

If you feel that you are being pressured into sexual acts or a sexual lifestyle with which you are not comfortable, take this as a warning for the whole of your relationship. If you are unable to discuss your discomfort with your partner, see your GP or access counselling for yourself. Do not just 'go along' with your partner as it will cause more distress to you in the long run.

The easy accessibility of pornography is blurring the boundaries of what previous generations might view as abnormal sexual expectations within a relationship. Porn addiction or sexual compulsivity is becoming an ever-increasing problem in relationships with some partners unable to experience satisfactory sex without its use. The sexual fantasy industry is making millions of pounds out of porn but is also undermining many otherwise happy and functioning relationships. We are not adopting a puritanical approach to the use of porn to spice up anyone's sex life but if we begin to view the fantasy of porn as our reality then we are our danger of destroying the chances of a satisfying long-term partnership. Always remember that the more porn is used by us the likelihood the nature of the acts depicted will have to become more and more extreme to stimulate our desire.

If your use or your partner's use of pornography is causing problems within your relationship psychosexual counselling is available and should be accessed through your GP.

Ask yourself:

1. Am I or my partner spending a significant portion of the day looking at pornography?

2. Are the images viewed altering my expectations of my sexual relationship?

3. Does my partner expect me to alter my appearance or sexual practices in any significant manner because of the influence of pornography?

4. Do I expect my partner to alter their appearance or sexual practices in any significant manner because of the influence of pornography?

5. Does my partner expect me to engage in sexual activity that feels to me physically or emotionally dangerous or shameful because of the influence of pornography?

6. Do I expect my partner to engage in sexual activity that my partner tells me feels physically or emotionally dangerous or shameful?

7. Have any of my previous relationships broken down because of my porn addiction/sexual compulsivity?

8. Have any of my partner's previous relationships broken down because of their porn addiction/ partner's sexual compulsivity?

***

Knowledge

At its most basic, sex is a mechanical, biological way for the human species to reproduce itself. Over the millennia different societies have taken this fundamental act and covered it up in layers of rules and laws, religious teaching and cultural expectations, producing myths, fears, truths and half-truths that help or hinder sexual satisfaction within our relationships. So how do we acquire the knowledge to allow us to give us the best chance of success to our sex life in a long-term relationship?

1. Don't listen to anyone else (unless they are a professional).
   People very rarely speak honestly about sexual matters so listen to yourself. Ask yourself: what is my sexual identity? What do I want to make me happy? Is my current sexual relationship making me happy?

2. Educate yourself.
   Whether you are just starting out in the relationship world or have been in a relationship for years, read good-quality books on sex. Trawl through your library, Amazon or a good-quality bookshop or the internet but beware of being led into porn sites.

3. Talk to your partner; listen to your partner.
   This may fill you with embarrassment and anxiety but what is worse? A bit of embarrassment or a lifetime of frustration? Make the time to talk privately with no children or other distractions around you.

4. Speak to your GP.
   If your sexual relationship is still unsatisfactory or you are struggling with your sexuality then your GP should be able to speak to you and can refer you to counselling services if necessary.

5. See a specialist.
   There are many clinical psychologists specialising in psychosexual and relationship problems, both in the NHS and privately. Speak to your GP for a recommendation.

Always remember: it is not acceptable for anyone to coerce, bully, belittle or threaten a partner into any sexual activity that feels innately wrong to them and such behaviour will negate a vital element of a sexual relationship; consent. Non-consensual sex has no part in a loving and trusting relationship. It's as simple as that.

And finally a word of caution: it is certain that in most cases what will not repair or enhance your sexual relationship with your partner is to have an affair.

****

Infidelity
'When a man marries his mistress it creates a job opportunity.'
—James Goldsmith

Figures for people admitting to extramarital sex vary wildly, with some surveys claiming that up to 70 per cent of married men and 50 per cent of married women have had an affair. Research has also shown that same-sex couples maybe more accepting of sex outside the relationship but on the whole being sexually faithful within a long-term relationship, whether married or not, is usually an unspoken but fundamental assumption in the relationship, even if one or other has a history of broken promises, unfaithfulness or multiple divorces.

Case Study

Jason and Meg have been married for five years. They met while both were married to other partners and had an affair that was exciting and highly sexually charged. Recently, Jason was devastated when he found that Meg has been accessing 'sex without strings' websites and meeting up with and having sex with strangers.

'My mother used to repeat the phrase, "How you get your man/woman is how you lose them," he says. 'And I should have listened. If she had an affair while she was married to Ron, her first husband, why did I think she'd be faithful to me?'

****

When we were in practice we often saw distraught wives, husbands or long-term partners who had found out their spouse or partner had had or was having an affair, or had used escort services or had had a one-night stand. And a common question we were asked was, Why?

'Why would my partner have an affair? We were so happy. Lots of money, fantastic social life, wonderful children and a good sex life. I just cannot understand it.'

****

The reasons why people have sex outside a committed relationship are many and varied. An often-quoted reason is that men use affairs to boost their self-esteem while women have affairs because they are bored. But over the years we heard many different reasons for infidelity: alcohol (office parties being an obvious culprit for many of those one-off incidents); unfulfilled high sex drive; chronic illness of one partner; wealth giving rise to increased opportunities; extensive travel for business giving rise to increased opportunities; lack of desire for a partner because of their weight gain; men blaming women because they concentrated on the children more than them; women blaming men because they concentrated on their careers more than them; and so it goes on.

It is a fact that some people are fundamentally incapable of being faithful to one partner. If the opportunity arises they will have short- or long-lived affairs. As with Chapter Four and conflict, we think that why people have affairs is in the main irrelevant. It is how each individual in the couple views infidelity that will determine whether the relationship will stand firm or collapse once infidelity has been discovered.

****

Working in certain environments can also increase the chances of affairs or serial one-night stands, particularly if a 'laddish' culture is encouraged. We are thinking of those parts of the financial services industry where the heady mix of money, alcohol and/or drugs (particularly cocaine), and late-night 'entertainment' have been the undoing of many a long-term relationship. Certain cultures may tolerate affairs (is it still true that in France 'cinq à sept' affairs are an accepted part of life?) and certain couples accept that affairs will be part of the relationship and will not end it.

'TV presenter Shaw Taylor faced embarrassment in 2004 when a former mistress, Sandy Kaye, sold her story to the *Mail On Sunday*. He made no comment but his wife Jane, unperturbed, declared in a separate interview: "'My husband's always been unfaithful. It started on our honeymoon." Obituary of Shaw Taylor, *The Times*, 19 March 2015

So, whatever the reasons may be for infidelity or what the consequences of infidelity, once revealed to the other partner, will be one thing is for sure. Even if the couple tolerates affairs or the affair does not cause the breakdown of the relationship, in most cases the trust element of the relationship will be forever damaged. And once trust has been damaged or destroyed, it will be very difficult to restore the relationship to a pre-affair level.

Ann Pearlman, a marriage and family therapist in the US, was stunned to discover that her husband, Ty, of thirty years was having an affair. In her book, *Infidelity: A Love Story*, she charts the breakdown of her relationship. She writes:

'The next morning, he continues the conversation as though we had never slept. "What is a limited-partnership marriage?"

"Like so many other marriages. An economic and companionate partnership with no expectations of intimacy or closeness."'

A limited-partnership marriage/relationship? It sounds so cold and business-like but one that is probably being played out in thousands of homes. How do we get from magically falling in love to a limited-partnership relationship and why would anyone want to stay in it?

****

Case Study

a. Ann and Rod meet at university and Ann falls deeply in love. They are inseparable for a year. One day, Ann's best friend telephones her and tells her that the previous night (when Ann had been revising in the library) she saw Rod kissing a fellow student at a club. Ann is devastated. When she confronts Rod he admits that he has been 'cheating on' Ann for several months but that it means nothing. He is deeply ashamed but could not resist the temptation when the other girl told him that she was attracted to him. Ann has a choice. She can tell Rod that it is over or she can forgive him and continue the relationship always feeling a little insecure about whether he will cheat on her again but hoping in time they can put the whole thing behind them. At this stage Ann need only think of herself, her own feelings and her own capacity to forgive and forget. She decides to finish the relationship because she cannot live with the feelings of insecurity.

b. Ann and Rod meet at university and they fall deeply in love. They are inseparable and when they get into their mid-twenties to the delight of both their families they marry. Both work in the insurance business, earning good incomes and bonuses. Eventually, they buy a home with a large mortgage and have two children now aged four and seven years. Ann gives up the commute into the city and gets a part-time local job so she can be with the children while Rod commutes three hours a day and spends a few weeks every so often travelling for business. While checking emails on the home computer, she comes across evidence that Rod has been accessing various porn sites and on digging further finds a file containing emails from an escort agency that shows Rod has used escort services.

Ann is devastated but now it is not as simple as considering her own feelings. Although she may be tempted to throw Rod out of the house and her life, she has the children to consider – they deserve a father. She has her financial future to consider – her earning power, constrained by child-care considerations, is not as high as it was and in the main she is financially dependent on Rod, She also has their respective families to consider – they will be equally devastated if the relationship breaks up.

When Ann confronts Rod with the evidence of his use of the escort agency he is at first angry and defensive – how dare she check his emails? And, anyway, he is bored with their lifestyle and she has become such a mummy that it is all her fault – but when he realises she is on the verge of finding out about a divorce he backtracks, agrees to go to couple counselling with her, and for the sake of the children they attempt to put it behind them. Ann never really trusts Rod again but as long as he is a good father and they manage to provide a comfortable upbringing for the children, she is happy(ish).

And, sadly, that's how most couples fall into a limited-partnership relationship.

Some of us may tolerate and forgive our partner's infidelity time and time again. Some of us may call an end to the relationship after one incident of unfaithfulness. None of us really knows what we might do until we are faced with the situation, but one thing is for sure: on learning that our partner has been unfaithful, most of us will question every aspect of our being.

In many circumstances it can be a relief to learn our partner had/is having an affair because at some level we know when a partner's attention has turned elsewhere. If we have confronted an unfaithful partner who will not admit guilt we may have been told we are mad or paranoid or pathetic or jealous. This is a particularly cruel form of mental torture and has been known to drive partners to the very brink of emotional instability.

But once we learn our suspicions were correct we will question everything. Our judgement – how could I have been so stupid/blind? Our attractiveness or desirability – am I so ugly/unattractive that they needed to have an affair? We will question our very sanity – am I going mad with distress or anger or jealousy? We will question how well we know ourselves – I am usually such a calm and placid person, so why am I plotting such terrible acts of revenge on my partner?

****

Case Study

Henry and Maisie married straight out of college, five years ago. At first they were very happy together. Their respective families paid off their student loans as a wedding gift, they had a fairy-tale wedding on the beach in Antigua and they both quickly landed graduate jobs. Within two years they had saved the deposit for a flat in their preferred area of

Bristol and they now live in a comfortable new-build within walking distance of their employment. Over the last year Maisie has seemed more and more distant towards Henry. They rarely make love, she spends several evenings a week out at client dinners and most weekends she prefers to go shopping with her sisters. Henry has become more and more upset that Maisie seems to be drifting away from him. He has asked her several times whether she is seeing someone else but she has denied this, saying Henry is suspicious and unreasonably jealous and that he is of putting pressure on her at a time when she is trying to work hard at her career.

A few weeks ago when he was at his office Henry received a telephone call from a woman claiming to be the wife of Maisie's boss. She told Henry that her husband and Maisie were having an affair and that she felt it was only fair that he knew. Henry was devastated. When he rang and told Maisie of what he had been told she denied everything but that night when she got home admitted that she had been having an affair and that she was leaving him. Henry begged Maisie not to leave but she did. He now feels that he humiliated himself by pleading. He veers from feeling almost murderous towards Maisie to spending all weekend crying because she has made it plain she is not coming back. 'It is like Maisie has died. Even if she came back we will never have the same closeness again. At times I hate her for the lying and cheating and using me as a mug. At others I just want her back. Sometimes, I think I'm going mad.'

Some of us (although it is rare) will tolerate affairs.

****

Case Study

Sophie and Rex have been together for three years. Rex is an extremely good-looking man with a high sex drive and while he and Sophie get on very well together he has slept with a number of other woman during their time together. Rex has always been open with Sophie about his affairs and curiously she says she feels no jealousy. Her take on the matter is that Rex will probably always have other relationships but that he will always come 'home' to her and that is enough for her.

If we were Sophie, at the very least we would be considering the chances of catching STDs, including HIV. Her tolerance could lead to serious health consequences for her in years to come. Sophie may also reconsider her approach if she has children with Rex.

Guidance

Be in no doubt that infidelity will change the nature of most relationships, the consequence of which may be a total relationship breakdown.

Infidelity can reach to the core of a person's mental health and in more than a few terrible cases an unfaithful partner has been murdered by a distraught rejected spouse/partner.

The following questions have no right or wrong answers but are intended to get you to think about your sexuality and your sexual relationship with your partner. Be as honest as possible.

1. During your childhood what were you told about sex?

2. Were you told that sex was shameful, dirty or sinful?

3. Are these childhood messages stopping you from enjoying a satisfying sex life with your partner?

4. Were you sexually abused in your childhood or the victim of rape or sexual assault? Have you accessed therapeutic help to overcome this trauma? Are these experiences stopping you from enjoying a satisfying sex life with your partner?

5. Have you found it necessary to hide your sexual identity from your family or community or partner?

6. How important is sex to you? Is it a fundamental or incidental part of a committed relationship?

7. Are you sexually compatible with your partner? Does one of you have a higher or lower sex drive than the other? How will this affect your long-term relationship?

8. Does anger, resentment or bitterness towards your partner inhibit a satisfactory sex life with them?

9. Have you been honest with your partner about any specific sexual preferences you may have or are you satisfying those preferences in secret?

10. Have you been pressurised into sexual acts or a sexual lifestyle that makes you feel ashamed or endangers your mental or physical health?

11. Can you talk freely with your partner about your sex life without embarrassment or conflict? Is sex a 'no-go' area for discussion? If so, why?

12. What would it mean to you if you found out that your partner had been unfaithful?

13. What would it mean to your partner if they found out that you had been unfaithful?

14. Would you be prepared to attend couple counselling to discuss sexual problems/infidelity within your relationship?

In our next chapter we will deal with something that can provoke more conflict, distress or upset than sexual problems and can trap people in long-dead relationships: money.

Chapter Seven
Money

When poverty comes in through the window,
love flies out of the door.'
—Anonymous

In our experience, the acquiring, spending or having access to money within relationships causes more distress and conflict than any other factor (including sex). The fear of losing a comfortable lifestyle or disrupting our financial security if we leave an emotionally dead or abusive relationship can trap us in it for years.

In all other areas discussed in this book there is little difference between couples who are married/in a civil partnership or who are unmarried but in a long-term committed relationship. The exception to this (and it is a big exception) is when we discuss money and financial matters in this chapter.

In England and Wales it is estimated that there are approximately two million unmarried cohabiting couples and we bet that a substantial proportion of them believe either that their relationship will be regarded as a 'common-law marriage' or that they will be in some way financially protected by the legal system if the relationship breaks down. *Wrong! Wrong! Wrong!*

***

Cohabitation or marriage: English law

Under English law there is no such thing as a 'common-law marriage' and as at 2015 cohabiting couples do not share the same legal rights as married/civil partnership couples, no matter how long we have lived together or how many children we have together. Moreover, if one partner in a cohabiting relationship dies without leaving a will, the remaining partner will not automatically inherit anything under the current intestacy rules.

If we marry or enter into a civil partnership then if the relationship breaks down and we cannot agree about the division of financial assets, the family courts of England and Wales can make various orders, including requiring the payment of income (maintenance) from one partner to the other (or for any children) or the payment of capital from one partner to the other or the transfer of property from one partner to the other or split pensions into two portions (pension sharing). This is regardless of who earned the money, owns the assets or even who is at 'fault' for the marriage/partnership breakdown. The family courts of England and Wales have no such powers if we are an unmarried couple. Also, if we are married/in a civil partnership and our spouse/partner dies without leaving a will, we will automatically be protected to a certain extent by the intestacy rules applicable in England and Wales, but not so if we are unmarried.

There may be myriad reasons why couples do not wish to marry but if we are going to have children together, commingle finances, build up businesses together, buy property together or decide to give up any source of our financial independence (including giving up work to look after children) then it is imperative we are aware of the financial consequences of our decisions.

As Erica Shelton, an experienced London family solicitor of Charles Russell Speechleys, says: '*Addressing the question of money with your partner at the beginning of a relationship can save a lot of heartache later on regardless of whether that relationship falters in the long run.*'

Case Study

Amy and Mark have known each other since sixth-form college and started going out with each other after Amy left university. Mark did not go to university but entered a large accountancy firm post-A level. Amy has substantial debt after university but Mark had been able to save for a large deposit and has bought a house (in his own name). Amy has begun teaching and slowly is paying off her debts. They live together in Mark's house. Amy and Mark maintain separate bank accounts, putting money into a joint account to pay the small mortgage and other household outgoings. Amy has no savings but Mark has inherited £20,000 on the death of an aunt. He is happy to pay for luxuries such as holidays and nights out, which Amy could not afford.

Amy and Mark marry and after five years they have two children aged three and one. They have agreed that Amy should take a career break until the children are older. Mark now pays a substantial part, but not all, of his income into the joint account. Amy does not know how much Mark has as savings in his name. Amy still has university loan debts and no savings.

Scenario 1

Mark suddenly announces that he has met someone else and that he wants a divorce. He says that Amy should get a job teaching again and move out of his house with the children so that he can move in his girlfriend. He will think about paying some maintenance for the children.

Amy goes to see a solicitor, who reassures her that if Mark will not come to a sensible agreement through negotiation or mediation the family courts will look at her and the children's needs regardless of the fact that the house and savings or pension entitlement are in Mark's name. The current starting point for the division of assets on the breakdown of a marriage/civil partnership is an equal division of all assets made from the time the couple started to live together and usually the marital home will be considered as a marital asset even if it was pre-acquired or purchased with non-marital assets. Amy issues divorce proceedings and eventually obtains an order that the house be sold and that she be given part of the proceeds to enable her to buy a new home for herself and the children. It's likely Mark will have to pay maintenance for the children and either a small amount over a short period to Amy until she gets back into teaching or other paid employment or joint lives maintenance if Amy can show, for some reason, she is not able to work. The family courts can interfere with Mark's capital and property ownership (including any pensions he may have) because the couple are married.

Scenario 2

The same facts but in these circumstances Mark has a heart attack and dies without leaving a will. Amy and the children are automatically protected by the intestacy rules and are entitled to make claims against Mark's estate. It is worth noting, however, that Amy will be entitled to inherit only up to £250,000 worth of Mark's assets with any remaining value split equally between Amy and the children. It would have been easier if Mark had made a will but with the help of a professional advisor Amy can sort things out.

Now, if we change one fact of the above, see how things could be entirely different – that is, the couple *never* married.

Scenario 1

Amy will have little or no claim in respect of the house unless she can show she has made a financial contribution to the mortgage or its upkeep. She will have no automatic claim in her own right on Mark's savings or his income or his pension as the family courts have no powers to make one unmarried partner transfer money/property to the other or to pension share. Because Amy has children with Mark she may have a potential claim against Mark for him to provide her with a home for her and the children until they finish full-time education but it will mean seeking professional advice. Also, unless Mark agrees to pay a level of maintenance for the children Amy will probably have to rely on the Child Maintenance Service (as from 2012) to obtain money for the children. This is not always a fail-safe method of getting reluctant parents to pay for their children's upkeep. In 2008 it was estimated that £3.8 billion was owed in child support payments.

Scenario 2
If Mark dies and does not leave a will, Amy will not automatically inherit any property or asset in his sole name. If Amy has been totally financially dependent on Mark she might be able to make a claim against his estate but as the children will probably inherit Mark's estate jointly under the intestacy rules it could leave Amy in the invidious position of making a claim against the children.

Whatever the outcome, by not being married at the time of Mark's death, under current English law Amy is in a very insecure financial position and risks having to pay large sums to a professional advisor to sort out any potential claims she may have, with no guarantee of success.

Guidance
If you do not intend to marry or enter into a civil partnership with your partner then we feel that it is essential you obtain legal or accountancy advice before you commingle finances, give up your financial independence or have children.

Even if your partner makes a will in your favour, remember that wills can be changed at any time. At the very least make sure that any property or assets purchased are in joint names or any financial contribution made by you is acknowledged in writing. It may be possible to enter into a 'cohabitation contract', agreeing the division of financial assets if the relationship breaks down. This can be done only with your partner's consent. This should be discussed with a specialist family solicitor.

We realise that whether or not we are married or in a civil partnership, when we fall in love, for most of us, anyway, the thought of tainting that love with grubby discussions about money seems abhorrent. The super-rich might enter into prenuptial contracts but if we have not got any money to start with or think involving lawyers before we begin a married life or a committed partnership is ridiculous, it will simply not enter our heads to sit down and talk sensibly about money at the beginning of our relationship. But we saw that money problems, disappointed expectations of the lifestyle we will enjoy with our partner, debts, failed businesses or a partner constantly in and out of work because of bad luck, health or addiction problems can cause more long-term conflict than any other aspect of our relationship. And at the end of a relationship what usually causes the most acrimonious wrangling? The division of money, of course.

Even being in a long-term relationship with someone whose wealth is disproportionately larger than ours can also cause problems later, particularly if their wealth is inherited or controlled by their family or family trusts. As we saw in Chapter Five, the 'other family' is generally reluctant to let any family money slide into the hands of a non-family member, whether or not they have been part of that family for many years (with or without children). If you are to marry someone with pre-existing wealth, you may be under pressure to enter into a prenuptial agreement. This will set out what would happen about money in the event the marriage broke down. It is vital you obtain advice from a specialist family solicitor before you enter into any such agreement.

There is a subtle balance of power even in the best of committed relationships and, in our experience, the single most influential factor in that balance will be money, whether it is earned, inherited or won on the lottery.

Case Study

Paula and Ralph have been married for twelve years. Both work but Paula, who is in finance, earns substantially more than Ralph, who is a paramedic. They have always had separate bank accounts, contributing to the mortgage and day-to-day expenses into a household account. Paula has more free income available for holidays and other luxuries and grudgingly pays for these from time to time. She is always at pains to remind Ralph that as she pays for the holidays it is her prerogative to choose where they go. If Ralph objects to her choice, Paula likes quoting the proverb 'He who pays the piper calls the tune' to him.

On the one hand Ralph enjoys holidaying in places that he could never afford on his salary. On the other hand he craves the freedom that total economic independence from Paula would bring and he bitterly resents being beholden to her, especially as he feels that his job is of more value to society than hers. Ralph has been having an affair with a work colleague on and off for a few years and if he is honest this is because in part it is his way of 'getting back' at Paula for thinking she holds the balance of power in the relationship because he does not earn as much as her.

***

People are usually very reluctant to discuss money matters and many of us will happily discuss the nuances of our sex lives before we will share secrets about what we earn, what assets we hold or what debts we have incurred, but our attitudes towards money can greatly influence the success or failure of our relationships. We need to discuss our attitudes towards money with our partner before we simply slide into a pattern of financial behaviour. We think that the best time to do that is not long after the one-year anniversary because by this time we will have established our spending patterns, probably discussed our expectations about lifestyle and living requirements (because it's going to take a lot more money to fund a flat and living in Central London than a croft on the Outer Hebrides) and we are not risking tainting the 'love drug' phase of our relationship with grubby chats about filthy lucre.

There are stories (which we hope are urban myths) of men and women researching who the top hedge-fund managers or other high-profile wealthy businessmen and -women are, and deliberately engineering meetings with them in the hope that they can be enticed into a relationship with the sole aim of extracting as much money as possible from the hapless victim. There are, of course, people around who will be looking for a 'walking wallet' and not much else, but for the majority of us it does seem hard-hearted and somewhat callous to sit down with our partner and force a conversation about money. Most of us ascribe to the passive 'let's see what happens' view of life and relationships rather than a proactive 'let's meet this head on' approach, but time and time again we saw the great anxiety, distress and worry that could be caused by fundamental differences between couples in attitudes towards money.

When we begin a long-term, committed relationship we become vulnerable emotionally, sexually and financially. We have to be prepared to trust our partner that not only will they be sexually faithful (if that is what we expect) but also that they will work with us to make a financially secure future for us and any children we may have together. Unless we earn, or have access to, lots of money and/or our partner's financial status means nothing to us, then if we entangle ourselves with a work-shy, feckless gambler our journey through life will be much, much harder than if we are with someone who is hard-working, financially solvent and honest.

A sensible discussion in the early days of our relationship about our approach to money, what money means to us, what future lifestyle we expect to enjoy together and how we will achieve that lifestyle could save a lot of upset later on.

Guidance
What you should think about and discuss:

1. At a suitable time (we suggest after a year in the relationship) you should have a full and frank discussion about your respective financial situations. Now is the time to discuss any property you may own, savings you may have, debts you have incurred, student loans, credit-card debts, store-card debts, etc. If this makes you or your partner feel uncomfortable or angry, ask yourself this: how can I trust or be trusted by my partner if they or I cannot be honest about our financial situation?

2. What are your financial expectations of the relationship? Do you intend to share equally any expenses, property, assets, or will one or either of you retain assets in your sole name even on marriage?

3. What lifestyle expectations do you have? How are these expectations to be achieved?

4. Do you expect your partner or are you expected to provide the financial basis of your relationship?

5. If you are planning to have children, will either one of you take a job/career break? How will you structure the financial basis of your relationship once you have children?

6. Is any money to be provided substantially by inherited or family/trust money? Should either of you be taking legal advice about your financial position in these circumstances?

7. In the event of marriage/civil partnership, will you expect or be expected to sign a prenuptial agreement? You should both obtain separate legal advice.

8. Are you fully aware of the different legal rights regarding assets/income or property if you are married/in a civil partnership or an unmarried couple? If your partner is not prepared to marry/ be in a civil partnership with you, and particularly if you have children or have commingled your finances, you should think of obtaining separate legal advice to possibly agree a 'cohabitation contract'.

9. If you are building up a business together, whether it be the local greengrocer's or a multimillion-pound venture, it is in your interests to seek legal and accountancy advice on how you can formally set out your respective duties/responsibilities/financial or other contributions you may be making to the business. That way there can be no argument at a later date about who did what.

10. Consider pension arrangements. It is still the case that many women, particularly if they compromised their earning power to care for children, have wholly inadequate pension provision, whereas men usually have a substantial pension provision on retirement. If a couple are married/entered into a civil partnership on retirement then a wife/husband can share in the pension; if widowed, more than likely she/he will be entitled to payments but not so if unmarried or not in a civil partnership. If married or in a civil partnership and divorcing, the courts can order pension sharing, not so if you split up and are unmarried or not in a civil partnership.

11. Consider income protection insurance for both or either one of you (married/in a civil partnership or not) to cover loss of income through illness.

12. Most of us have files containing our financial records – utility bills, bank statements, credit cards. Added to that we suggest that once every year you review your finances, your financial objectives and lifestyle choices. It is important

not to slip into financial decisions without being fully aware of any consequences. It might be sensible to have a 'relationship finance file', noting down any major financial decisions/contributions you make during the relationship. It is interesting to see how often two people after the passage of time can forget conversations or agreements about major financial matters.

The above may not seem so relevant if you have been together for years but if the financial side of your relationship is causing problems we suggest you seek professional help, either from a solicitor or an accountant. If debt has become a problem within the relationship there are many debt-counselling agencies and your local Citizens Advice Bureau should be able to refer you.

***

It is also vital at whatever stage you are in your relationship to obtain legal advice in the following circumstances:

1. If your partner is self-employed or runs a business and you are being asked to secure business or personal debts on any property or asset owned jointly or solely by you.

2. If you are asked by your partner to re-mortgage your home or other assets to secure loans to pay for anything but particularly high-risk investments like start-up businesses/playing the stock market/buying second foreign homes or expensive boats

or cars or anything that will lose value as soon as it is purchased. You must think very carefully and obtain advice if asked to sign documentation for loans to any third party or give loans to your partner for anything that could drastically diminish your current financial situation.

3. If you are married/in a civil partnership and asked by your spouse to sign a postnuptial contract. This is an agreement drawn up after marriage that sets out how a couple's finances would be split in the event of divorce, separation or upon death. These are rare but it is essential you seek legal advice if you are under pressure from a spouse to sign a postnuptial contract.

4. If your financial situation is reliant on your partner's inherited or family trust money and you are asked to sign any documentation without a clear understanding of the financial consequences.

5. If your partner is moving family/personal money to a foreign jurisdiction, whether or not you are being assured that it is for 'tax-planning purposes'.

6. In any circumstances, if you feel that you do not have a clear understanding of the financial basis of your relationship and your partner will not provide a clear and adequate explanation, seek legal advice.

Guidance

If we participate with our partner in a lifestyle that we know is funded by criminality or we turn a blind eye to dodgy dealings, tax evasion or shady business practices, do not be surprised if, when the relationship comes to an end, your partner does not play fair where money is concerned. A 'smoke and mirrors' lifestyle can disappear in an instant once a relationship falters, leaving embittered ex-partners futilely scrambling for evidence of income/capital/property.

Our approach to money and what it means to us will be influenced by our own personality traits, childhood experiences, our ability and talent to earn money and, perhaps more importantly, to hold on to money, our access to inherited/family money, our personal philosophy about money, and external circumstances such as economic downturns, health issues and downright bad luck.

We saw five basic personality traits that underpinned a person's attitude towards money, whether or not there was a lot of or little money around.

1. The 'Scrooge'

This personality type is not necessarily mean-spirited but they will be aware of the cost of every meal out, holidays, clothes, household expenses, presents and so on, and usually an exact repayment from their partner for their share will be expected. They will give little meaning to anything within the relationship that cannot be given a *monetary value*. They will be resistant to opening joint accounts and will probably only agree to the purchase of a property in joint names because they need the other partner's salary to be taken into account for the mortgage. They will keep a scrupulous eye on expenditure within the relationship and although it is unlikely that debt or risky financial investments will be a problem with the 'Scrooge' type, their caution and lack of generosity will make some partners feel trapped in an uncaring relationship.

The 'what's mine is mine' approach to money within a relationship will work as long as both parties are more or less on an equal financial footing. Problems will occur if one has to become financially dependent on the other because of long-term illness, unemployment or child care. If you are with someone who tends towards the 'Scrooge' type then you must think carefully about taking out income protection insurance in case of unemployment or illness, and if you are giving up work temporarily or permanently to cover child care then think very carefully about the financial implications for you.

Case Study

Theo and Geoff have been together for seven years. They live together in a jointly owned flat and each have their own bank accounts while contributing equally to the mortgage or expenses. Geoff, who works as a landscape gardener, has no idea what Theo earns as a lawyer for a large international law firm. Theo made it clear when they first got together that he expected Geoff to contribute equally to any holidays, household costs, food bills, restaurant/theatre trips, cars, etc. At the end of the month Theo presents Geoff with an itemised bill of their expenditure and either one will repay the other if there is a shortfall on one side or the other.

This has worked well over the years but recently Geoff has been diagnosed with MS. Geoff may not be able to continue to work. He has no income protection insurance and little savings. Theo has made it clear to Geoff that although he is happy to look after him, if the disease progresses he will expect Geoff to sign over to him his interest in the flat if he is to financially support Geoff. Geoff is very upset and feels that Theo is being heartless. Theo sees it as a logical and perfectly fair way of dealing with the situation. 'I thought being in a relationship meant we supported each other in sickness and in health,' says Geoff. 'It's all down to money with Theo.'

2. The generous type

'For all his wealth and success, Lazari never lost sight of what he considered to be the most valuable things in his life. "Family for me means a lot more than money. If money is only a token of success in one's work, then a good happy family is the token of success in one's life. I am a simple man at heart because simple things in life give me much more pleasure than luxuries."' Obituary of Christos Lazari, *The Times*, 6 August 2015

Having a generous nature has nothing to do with the amount of money a person earns or has access to. Someone who is generous with money will usually also be generous with their love, affection and time. They will not be interested in keeping a running total of what they have spent on their partner or for their benefit but prefers to think that it will all even out in the end. They will probably be more than happy to run joint accounts, buy property in joint names and on the whole have a relaxed attitude to money. They do run the risk of being taken advantage of by someone who prefers the 'Scrooge' approach and they need to be self-disciplined about incurring debt. It's all very well being generous with money but it is not such an appealing trait if it leads to unmanageable debt or diminishing income or capital assets.

Case Study

Marcie and George have been married for twenty years and have three teenage children. George is a social worker and Marcie a nurse. Although they both work hard they do not have a huge joint income but Marcie and George have always been very generous with money by helping close friends in financial difficulties, supporting several charities with monthly donations and making sure that the family has nice holidays, clothes and treats. They are not so generous, however, that they overspend and have always agreed a budget and make sure that any major financial decisions are discussed and agreed between them. 'We could have saved more,' says George, 'but we want our family and friends to know they can rely on us to help in difficult times and that is important to us both.'

George and Marcie have a shared understanding that money simply for its own sake will not make them happy. They value the joy that the love and respect of their family and friends brings them.

3. The 'Mr Micawber' type

In *David Copperfield* by Charles Dickens Mr Micawber's guiding principle is, 'Something will turn up.' We would add 'or somebody' to that. The Mr (or Ms/Mrs) Micawbers of this world don't plan financially and will generally be in debt, having spent money on holidays, cars, new shoes or handbags, entertainment or whatever catches their fancy at the moment. They are experts at applying for new credit cards, fantasising about the big win on the lottery or hoping that they can attract a financially solvent partner.

If they are high earners they will be always looking to the next bonus or the next business deal to fund their high-rolling lifestyles, which will generally work unless they are affected by economic downturns or illness. The 'Mr Micawber' types are usually fun to be with but unless we are very lucky be prepared for a lifetime of financial uncertainty if we are with them on a long-term basis. It is probably best to maintain some financial independence from them if we want to keep control over our finances long term.

Case Study

When Pete, a self-employed shopfitter, met Sara, a local boutique owner, he loved the fact that she was lots of fun, well dressed and groomed, drove an expensive sport car and gave every impression of being a successful businesswoman. In their first year together they took lots of foreign holidays and ate out nearly every night, with Sara happy to pay her share of the costs. Pete was hopeful that Sara would agree to move in with him and that they would eventually marry. On one particular weekend, when Sara was away with girlfriends, she asked Pete to feed her cat and gave him the keys to her flat. When Pete went to the flat he fed the cat and opened the refuse bin to throw away the cat-food container, and was puzzled to find hundreds of pounds' worth of used scratch cards thrown in it.

When Sara returned from her trip he tentatively asked her why he had found so many scratch cards. At first Sara was very angry with Pete and accused him of spying on her but then broke down and confessed that she had enormous credit-card debts and business loans and that the only way she could think of to get enough money together was to win it. Pete considered walking away from the relationship, particularly as he had a horror of debt, but instead asked Sara if she would let him look at her full financial situation and let him help her. Sara agreed to contact a debt counselling agency, Pete agreed to give her some money from his savings and together they managed to work out a budget to enable Sara to get back into control of her finances. Pete, however, felt that his trust in Sara had taken a hefty knock and although he still hoped they would have a long-term future together he was determined to keep his finances separate from Sara's.

4. The worrier type

No matter how much money is around, if we are a 'worrier' type there will never be enough. Impending bankruptcy and financial ruin are just a step away for the worrier. This anxiety will probably be rooted in a childhood where poverty or unpredictability about finances dominated the family. The worrier might present as a 'Scrooge' type but they might not necessarily be ungenerous, it's just that they will see the acquisition of money as a protection against the gut-churning anxiety and chaos of poverty. The worrier's favourite question to a partner will be, 'But can we afford it?'

The worrier type is probably risk averse and it may be difficult to get them on board with speculative property buying or investments. Constant worry about money, whether real or not, can cause anxiety in long-term relationships and if you or your partner is a worrier then it is probably sensible to discuss your financial situation and financial objectives every few months or so. The worrier needs the tangible evidence of bank statements, spreadsheets and so on to satisfy themselves all is well financially.

Case Study

Nora comes from a large family of seven children, with parents who were in and out of work on a regular basis. Loan sharks and bailiffs were regular visitors to the family home when she was a child. Nora was lucky as she was a clever child and managed to get to university, where she studied economics and has been a high-flying and well-paid executive at a bank for many years. She is married to Ted and has two children. Despite the fact that Ted and Nora have been very sensible and astute with money, live in a large house (mortgage-free) and send the children to private schools, Nora is plagued with anxiety about their financial situation. She still shops for clothes in the sales, buys food at cut-price supermarkets and is reluctant to 'waste money' on holidays and other treats. From time to time Ted feels exasperated with Nora as she never seems to be able to relax and enjoy their hard-earned money and her anxiety clouds their relationship. This causes arguments, which makes Nora very unhappy.

5. The secretive type

The secretive type will brook no discussion with a partner about money. There will be no discussion of their financial position. Indeed, the more money a partner who is secretive may have the more likely it is tied up offshore or owned by shell companies or complicated trusts. The secretive type is suspicious of everyone, particularly an intimate partner who they feel may eventually take them to the cleaners financially. Indeed, it is more than likely that the secretive type will have been married before and lost money in a divorce. They will be very reluctant to commit to marriage or entangle their finances with a new partner (whether they have had children or not with their new partner) as they will be determined to protect their money at all costs.

Even if the secretive type is not overly wealthy they will be extremely reluctant to apprise their partner of any financial details. A good degree of cynicism is at the heart of this character and their love of money and its accumulation will generally override any potential for a truly loving relationship. A relationship with someone who is secretive about money will inevitably lack trust, which will surely cause arguments and eventually cause many such partnerships to destabilise. It is likely the secretive type will move from relationship to relationship never really committing fully to a truly intimate partnership.

Case Study

Naomi is single, in her late forties, a successful businesswoman and the head of an international organisation. She met Nicholas, a divorcee, at a business conference six years ago and since then they have met several times a week for dinner or the theatre, spent holidays together and generally get on well. They maintain separate homes in London but spend a few nights a week together at one or the other's place. Nicholas is vague about his wealth although it is obvious to Naomi that he has access to large sums to maintain his lifestyle. Nicholas has hinted on a few occasions that his ex-wife and children live in somewhat reduced circumstances as he had successfully hidden most of his wealth abroad long before the divorce occurred. The fact that his children are not well provided for by Nicholas seems not to bother him at all. Naomi is an astute businesswoman and realises the limitations of the relationship. This relationship functions perfectly well on a superficial basis but Naomi feels that she cannot really trust Nicholas and that the relationship lacks the depth that she feels is essential in a truly loving partnership.

****

Our childhood experiences with money will influence our attitudes to money. If, like Nora, we have known poverty or uncertainty about money in our childhood, the acquisition and retention of money can become all-consuming, to the cost of our relationship. If we have benefited from family comfort or wealth we might find it hard to value money for its own sake or not be particularly ambitious to make money, believing that it will always 'turn up'. In time we all develop personal philosophies about money. Is the love of money the 'root of all evil' or is money a necessary tool that enables us to be free to make our own choices about our lives? Again, fundamental differences between couples and our philosophy about money and the acquisition of it can cause real problems in the relationship. This usually comes down to how motivated we are to acquire money or how able we are to make it. We might be very motivated but just do not have the talent or luck to make it, or we may not be motivated at all.

***

The following questions are intended to be self-reflective or provoke a conversation with your partner. Which statements below do you or your partner agree with?

1. I am ambitious to make money to fulfil long-held dreams of a particular lifestyle.

2. I am ambitious to make money as I want people to see how successful I have become.

3. I am ambitious to make money as I want to be able to provide security for myself and/or my family as best as I can.

4. I am ambitious to make money as I have had the uncertainty of debt/poverty in my childhood.

5. I am ambitious to make money as I like the power or control it can give me over my partner, family, friends or business colleagues.

6. I am ambitious to make money as I am acquisitive by nature.

7. I am ambitious to make money but I feel I do not have the skills or talents to enable me to have a high earning capacity.

8. I am ambitious, do not have a high earning capacity but I expect my partner to provide material comfort for me.

9. I am not particularly ambitious to make money:

   a. for spiritual reasons;

   b. for alternative lifestyle reasons;

   c. because I have sufficient earned or inherited wealth;

   d. because I am unable to work because of long-term health problems or other reasons;

   e. because I am not motivated by money and am happy working with little or no responsibility.

10. I share my partner's philosophy and attitudes towards money.

11. I expect my partner to be as ambitious as me.

12. I am not concerned if my partner is not as ambitious as I am or is unable to contribute equal money to the relationship.

13. I do not think that two partners within the same relationship can be equally ambitious. One will have to scale down their ambitions to support the other.

14. I would/would not expect my partner (if necessary) to give up their career/job to support my career.

15. I would/would not be prepared to give up my career/job to support my partner's career/job.

16. I expect my partner to contribute equally to any expenditure within the relationship.

17. I expect my partner and I to become a 'life team', supporting each other financially each according to his/her own abilities throughout our relationship, whatever the circumstances.

18. I would/would not be happy or be unable to financially support my partner if he/she became chronically ill/unemployed.

19. I would/would not expect my partner to return to work after the birth of children.

20. I would/would not be happy or be unable to support my partner after our children are born.

21. I would/would not be happy to be a stay-at-home parent after the birth of our children.

22. I have no intention of commingling my finances with my partner or allowing my partner to have any information about my wealth.

****

Our financial circumstances will inevitably change for the better or worse during the life of our relationship. Money can be made through sheer guts, determination and hard work, it can be gained by luck or chance or inherited, but it can also just as easily be lost through ill health, financial irresponsibility, laziness or a bad throw of the dice.

Under no circumstances, unless we are happy to risk financial insecurity at a later date, should anyone in a long-term relationship (particularly if we are not married) sit back and let our partner earn, accumulate, manage or control the whole of the money in the relationship. We should begin our financial relationships as we begin the emotional side of our relationships, with realism, honesty, self-awareness and with knowledge of the legal and practical consequences of any financial decisions we may make. As long as we are clear-sighted about money and its impact on our relationship, it should not present too many problems later.

Chapter Eight
Children

"I would have been a terrible mother because I'm basically a very selfish human being. Not that that has stopped most people going off and having children."
—**Katherine Hepburn, from** *Kate Remembered*
by A. Scott Berg

We can imagine that some of you may have drawn in a sharp intake of breath when you read the above, particularly if you are in the first throes of a new, loving relationship. After all, most of us accept that when we find our true love and settle down into a committed relationship we will have children together. There is something deep down within most of us that makes us feel we cannot be complete as a family until we have children.

But having children is not necessarily part of everyone's life plan and if it is not then it is only fair to discuss this with our partner at an early stage in the relationship; we would say certainly within the first year. Many people cannot contemplate not having children at some stage and being with a partner who does not want children (as opposed to a partner who is unable to have children) will usually be a deal-breaker. This is the time for a conversation of complete honesty. It is also the time for being realistic. People do change their minds but if we are with a partner who is clear that they do not want children then continually hoping that they will change their minds or worse (if we are female) becoming 'accidentally' pregnant will, unless we are very lucky, undoubtedly lead to trouble.

When my husband and I married, we both saw ourselves as ambivalent about having children. Since then, aside from a brief interlude of semi-willingness, my ambivalence had slid into something more like opposition. Meanwhile, my husband's ambivalence had slid into abstract desire. A marriage counsellor would surely advise a couple in such a situation to discuss the issue seriously and thoroughly, but, wrenching as it was not to be able to make my husband happy in this regard, it seemed to me there was nothing to discuss. I didn't want to be a mother; it was as simple as that.
—*The Unspeakable* by Meghan Daum, 2014

We are fortunate to live in the West in the twenty-first century because we have access to contraception, giving us the choice of having or not having children and, unless we are part of a community or culture that frowns on having children outside marriage, there are now few societal objections to children born out of wedlock or born to same-sex couples. With the availability of IVF, surrogacy, adoption, both home based and international, donor egg provision, sperm donation (and so on), our age, sexual orientation, and an inability to conceive naturally have become more and more irrelevant. In the UK in 2013 approximately 2,010 babies were born to women over the age of forty-five and, indeed, in an increasing number of cases even being in any relationship has become irrelevant as women decide to go through IVF alone. In 2013, 952 single women registered at fertility clinics in the UK.

We have made no distinction in the following chapter between children conceived naturally or children becoming part of a family after adoption or medical intervention. As an aside we would say that if you are considering a surrogacy arrangement you should obtain specialist legal advice before you enter into any agreement, pay over any money or take steps for the surrogate to be impregnated as surrogacy agreements are not currently binding in England and Wales and they cannot be enforced.

****

If you are in a relationship and are considering having children, our guidance from Chapter One is worth repeating: *If at all possible it is wise to live with your partner for at least a year without making any major life decisions such as marrying, having a child or entwining your financial affairs.*

It is an inescapable fact that once we have a child with our partner, whether or not the relationship survives we will be forever bound to that person through our child(ren). As we have said previously, entering into a committed relationship makes us vulnerable emotionally, sexually and financially, and this vulnerability will be magnified tenfold once we have a child.

It is also an obvious statement (although one that a lot of us seem to forget when the urge to have a child comes upon us) that choosing the right partner with whom to have our children is one of the most important things we will do in our life for ourselves and our child(ren). This is not only because we should be trying to give any child the best possible chance of love and happiness in their lives but also because although most children in the UK are born into two-partner relationships it seems that one in four dependent children ends up living in a lone-parent home, having experienced the disintegration of the parental relationship. It is interesting to note that research seems to suggest, in the UK anyway, that cohabiting parents are more likely to separate than married parents. We are not sure why this is so but perhaps getting married shows a greater commitment to the relationship, which does not so easily buckle under the strain of having children.

****

In our introduction to this book we said that more thought seems to be given to buying a car or agreeing a phone contract than entering into a relationship, and we would extend that to having children. Once we become parents we become not only the custodians of our children's future but to an extent that of our descendants. We only have to read any one of the hundreds of available 'misery memoirs' to know how parents can blight their children's lives, the effect of which can trickle down the generations.

So it's not that every second of my childhood was filled with doom. But every second was filled with the possibility that in an instant my father's mood would plunge into irrationality, rage and ultimately violence. This very feeling, this possibility, is what darkens the part of my mind where my childhood stories live.

—*Not My Father's Son* by Alan Cumming

It should be very simple. If we are not ready to have a child for whatever reason, then don't, no matter what the external pressures.

Other than the simple biological urge to reproduce, what should we be considering if we want (by which we mean becoming pregnant/adopting/having a child by a surrogate, etc.) a child with our partner? We recognise that there may be gender differences in the answers to the questions below – women may well have a greater hormonal impetus to want/parent children – but on the whole, except where stated, there should be no particular gender bias. Ask yourself (and then your partner):

1. *Why* do I want to have a child?
Is your relationship rocky and you feel that having a child will save it? Is it because your family or community expects you to have a child? Are you ambivalent about having a child but your partner wants one? Do you see having a child as a way of getting out of a hated job or career or enhancing your status within a family or community?
If the honest answer is 'yes' to any of the above questions then a healthy dose of realism is needed as

it is certain having a child will almost never keep a relationship together or produce a magical solution to a difficult situation. In fact, it is more likely to place added emotional and financial pressure on even the most of committed and loving partnerships. On having a first child it's likely you will feel exhausted, anxious, bored and frustrated in equal measure, although hopefully this will run alongside a fierce, protective love, the depth of which most of us thought we would never experience. The heady mix of anxiety, sleep deprivation, the burden of extra financial responsibility and work or possible ambivalence about whether we or our partner want children can put intolerable pressure on even the most loving partnership, let alone one that is under strain anyway. A German study based on 20,000 participants showed that '...*the drop in "life satisfaction" following the birth of a first child was worse than that caused by redundancy, divorce and even bereavement.*' *Daily Telegraph*, 6 August 2015

Case Study

Marnie and Paul are in their late twenties and have been together for three years. They have had a tempestuous relationship and have broken up four times for short periods during their time together. When they reunited on the last occasion Paul was adamant that they should begin a family. He felt they were clearly meant for each other and that the introduction of a baby would seal their relationship.

'We need to grow up and a baby will help us do that,' he said. Marnie was slightly sceptical about whether it was right to get pregnant but caved in to Paul after a few months. Baby Toby was born prematurely at thirty-two weeks and has been weak and sickly ever since. He is now fourteen months old, much loved but is very demanding of Marnie's time and energy. Marnie feels exhausted, always anxious about Toby's health and has no time to deal with Paul and his constant demands that they 'reclaim their sex and social lives'.

'I've grown up all right,' says Marnie, 'and I can now see Paul very clearly as a selfish man who can only think of his own needs.'

Marnie has moved out of their home and is now back with her parents, who are willing to provide loving care for her and Toby. Marnie is honest and says that she even though she deeply loves Toby she regrets going along with Paul's assurances that a child could repair their difficult relationship.

****

There is no doubt that having children can be very rewarding and fulfilling but if we want to look after our children as best we can then we have to dig deep into our emotional resources to love unconditionally and with an inevitable degree of self-sacrifice. If we are honest with ourselves some of us are simply not able to do this. If we are agreeing to have a child to please another's expectations or that of our community or to satisfy our own selfish needs, can we really be committed emotionally to that child? The common teenage cry of 'I didn't ask to be born' is as true as it is infuriating to most parents. They really did not ask to be born so why bring them into this world on a half-hearted whim?

It is also important to be very honest about the quality of our relationship when considering why we want to have a child with our partner. In particular, how we resolve conflict in our relationship can have a huge effect upon our child(ren). It can be very frightening for children to experience their parents' volatility (the nuclear over-reactors), although we are sure that it can be just as upsetting for children to live in an emotionally cold and distant household.

****

After a year living together (if we have been lucky enough to have been able to achieve this) we should be able to take a good hard look at the quality of our relationship and consider whether we are or our partner is 'parent material'. We realise this sounds a tad cold, calculating even, especially when anyone having a child makes a huge leap of faith, but some thought and discussion with our partner at this stage can prevent considerable distress and upset later.

Some of us simply do not view having a family as a positive step in our lives but see it as boring, too grown up and downright claustrophobic. If you (or your partner) sees life as more *Sex and the City* than *The Waltons* then be honest! If we are able to sit down with our partner and honestly discuss why we wish/do not wish to have a child then we may decide that our adult relationship is enough, or we may have doubts about our partner's suitability as a parent, or happily we will feel that we are both ideally suited to the joint venture of parenthood. Whatever the outcome of our discussions, if we have both been honest, any children we do have will have been brought into the world with at least a fighting chance of a loving childhood provided by two committed parents.

2. What does having a child mean to me (or my partner?)
Having a child can mean many things to us, not just the physical representation of our love for our partner. It can be oppressive as it means the end of a responsibility-free existence, it can be challenging as it means we have to suppress our own wants and desires as they take a back seat to another's needs, or it can be downright threatening as another human being takes the attention of our partner away from us. A surprising number of heterosexual men have affairs/one-night stands while their partner is pregnant. It could be that this infidelity is motivated by a combination of all three factors above but, whatever the cause, most women will find it very difficult to forgive such a gross breach of trust at a time when she is obviously at her most vulnerable.

One theory is that having a child means that we have an opportunity to 're-parent' ourselves. We make up for deficiencies in our own childhood by giving our child things that we feel were missing for us. This is where a degree of self-awareness comes in handy. In having a child, are we trying to make up for gaps in our own childhood? Will this approach really help our children, who after all are not 'us reborn'?

Case Study

James and Mark have two teenage children, Marley and Jake, both born to a surrogate mother. James is the prime carer for the children while Mark runs his own successful PR company. James has a close relationship with his parents and enjoyed a comfortable upbringing. Mark has a cold and distant relationship with his widowed father. Mark was brought up in a council home where money as well as love and affection was in short supply. He and James only ever argue about Mark's over-the-top spending on clothes, gifts and entertainment or holidays for the children as Mark cannot say no to the children if they ask him for anything. James is keen to instil in the children a respect for money by giving them pocket money for doing chores and encouraging them to save for treats. But Mark says, 'My father gave me nothing either financially or emotionally. That's not going to happen with my boys. I want them to have what I didn't.' The boys are beginning to adopt a careless and spendthrift attitude towards money but James feels he is powerless to influence them while Mark refuses to stop spoiling them.

Having children can also be an attempt to replicate our own childhood experience.

Case Study

Marina, an artist, is the sixth child of eight brothers and sister. Her childhood was very loving but quite noisy and chaotic. Jes, an estate agent, is an only child. He also had a warm and loving childhood. Marina and Jes have been together for two years and have one child already. Marina has made it very clear that she would like lots more children and cannot contemplate only having one or two. Jes is constantly worried about how they will financially support lots of children. He has found their first child exhausting and is highly anxious about having any more. His idea of a happy family is one or at a push two children in a calm, quiet and financially stable environment. Marina's idea of heaven is lots of children, lots of noise and chaos. Her view is that her parents were able to successfully muddle through so why won't she and Jes?

Perhaps it would have been better for Jes and Marina to have discussed their expectations of how many children they wanted before they began to have children together.

3. Who will be the main carer for our child(ren)?
Even if we do not want to think about why we want a child or what it means to us, anyone considering having a child must consider and discuss the ever-thorny question of who will provide child care. Will we both work and rely on grandparents for child care, or have a nanny, an au pair or obtain nursery care? Will one of us have a temporary or permanent career break to care for the children?
Some writers see the division of child care as firmly slewed in favour of the male corner, with women's economic independence particularly being affected by having children. Indeed, the website www.pregnantthenscrewed.com claims that around 54,000 women a year in the UK are forced out of their jobs because they are pregnant.

****

Parenting demands compromise, it demands the 'work of love'. It is the price we pay for a richer life and a fulfilling relationship with our children. But this price is paid disproportionately by women. Their responsibility for family life restricts the other aspects of their existence. Women do not have the opportunity to develop their careers, public roles or personal interests to the same degree as men because they take on the work of the private sphere in a way fathers do not. They suffer a consequential reduction in their economic worth, independence and social status and experience their power in the relationship diminish. Dependent on their partners for money and status, women are sitting ducks.
—*Shattered: Modern Motherhood and the Illusion of Equality* Rebecca Asher

We found that a lot of the literature discussing the consequences on couples of having children does tend to focus on what happens to women within heterosexual relationships with little account taken of what happens when men decide to become 'house-husbands'.

'In years gone by, the likelihood that a woman would find herself earning more than her husband was minuscule. A 'woman's place', though no longer necessarily in the home, was typically not as main breadwinner – even a generation ago. Yet, slowly, subtly, the economic and cultural climate has changed, and this week (May 2015) a report for insurers LV found that a quarter of young women now out-earn their partners. —*Daily Telegraph*, 1 May 2015

So, as women begin to out-earn their partners and more and more men are taking temporary or permanent career breaks to care for the family, will 'house-husbands' suffer the same reduction in their economic worth and power within the relationship as women report? And what happens when one partner within a same-sex relationship with children takes on the lion's share of child care?

We would say that the partner maintaining their place in the work environment, whatever their sex, will inevitably not suffer the consequences of taking temporary or permanent career breaks and will, therefore, be able to earn more money on a long-term basis than the partner who provides the bulk of the child care. Whether this becomes an issue within the relationship is down to the particular relationship dynamic.

****

We do not see that the problem nowadays is as simple as men versus women. The actual problem is caused by the lack of value placed on child care and home-making by the individuals within the relationship and society as a whole, whether or not the bulk of the child care/home-making is carried out by men or women (either in heterosexual or other types of relationship).

Going out to work every day to provide for a family is hard and challenging but it is also financially rewarding and, if we are successful, personally gratifying, whereas attending to children is also hard and challenging but on the whole not financially rewarding or necessarily personally gratifying. Anecdotally, we have been told by practising matrimonial lawyers that some of the most bitter relationship breakdowns are between high-earning career women and their house-husbands/partners.

The fact that their husbands/partners have been put in an old-fashioned female role where their career prospects and earning capacity have been diminished severely by child-care responsibilities cuts no ice with them at all. The women, as the main breadwinners, are adopting a certain time-honoured traditional male perspective towards their partners. The 'I earned it. He just sat at home playing with the kids. Why should I have to give him a penny?' attitude. This reinforces our feeling that the difficult consequences within a relationship attendant on having children are not just because of a male/female divide.

****

It is the partner (of either sex) who bites the bullet and jeopardises their earning power by taking time out to care for children who puts themselves in a far more vulnerable position if the relationship breaks down at a later date. Similarly, they can be just as vulnerable within the relationship if they have chosen to have children with a partner who consistently undervalues family life or subscribes to the 'He who pays the piper calls the tune' philosophy of life.

There is no doubt that any romantic fantasies we may hold of family life will be severely tested by the reality so being honest, clear-sighted and self-aware about the quality and nature of our relationship before having children is highly desirable.

All those idiotically lyrical articles about sharing child-rearing duties never mention that, nor do they allude to something else that happens when a baby is born, which is that all the power struggles of the marriage have a new playing field.

—Nora Ephron

As we saw in Chapter Seven, our attitudes towards money will undoubtedly affect the quality of our relationship and any differences in those attitudes between us and our partner will be brought into sharp relief once we have children together. As we said, the 'What's mine is mine' approach to money will work for as long as both partners are on an equal financial footing. But what happens when one decides to (or has to) reduce their earnings to deal with children? What happens if it is true that pregnant women are eased out of many workplaces with devastating financial consequences? The 'Scrooge' type will have to be shown the hard value of the stay-at-home (either permanently or temporary) child carer/home-maker and the 'worrier' will have to be assured that having children will not bankrupt the family.

Guidance

Before you have children speak to a local nursery with a good reputation.

How much will full-time monthly child care cost? How much would a local cleaner/laundry service cost? This should be noted down in your 'Relationship Finance File' as this is the basic value of a stay-at-home partner.

It is vital we sit down with our partner before we have a child to discuss who will provide the main care for children as the economic basis of our relationship may have to be recalibrated when we have children. We feel that this should not only be discussed but also recorded in our 'Relationship Finance File'. As circumstances change, any decisions can be revisited but at least recording who agreed what in respect of child care can give you a good reference point for future discussions (or arguments).

Consider the following questions in your discussion:

1. Will we both work?
2. Who will look after our children if we both work? Parents, a nanny, an au pair or nursery?
3. Will either of you work from home? How will child care and work commitments at home be structured?
4. If we will both work, what is the cost of child care? Will this be paid by one or both of us?
5. If one partner is to stay at home (part time or full time), how will this affect their job/career prospects?
6. Will the stay-at-home partner be expected or expect to resume work after a period of time?
7. How will we manage our finances after our child is born? Will the stay-at-home partner be expected to be financially dependent on the other partner?
8. How will child-care responsibilities be divided?

Who will take/collect children from nursery/ school, help with homework, bathe, read stories, take children to parties, etc.? We have heard of couples who write down every minute they spend with the children and do a weekly reckoning up so that if one partner has done more they are credited with that time, which the other has to make up. This seems to be a rather over-scrupulous approach to the division of child care but at least no one can feel that they are being taken advantage of!

9. How will school holidays be covered by us if we both work?

10. Who will pay for costs for the children – clothes, entertainment, holidays, gifts, etc.? Will this be paid by one or both of us?

11. How will household chores be divided, particularly if we both work? Interestingly, research has shown that there is a higher risk of divorce if men fail to share child care and housework, but if they do share household tasks, including child care, reported long-term sexual satisfaction is higher. As we highlighted in Chapter Four, petty acts of thoughtlessness or lack of regard will over time vastly erode and undermine the quality of a relationship (inevitably leading to less sexual satisfaction) and being treated as an unpaid skivvy in our own home must be one of the more irritating acts of thoughtlessness!

12. How much importance do you or your partner place on the creation of children and a family home?

13. Are you or your partner able to see the value (not in monetary terms) of creating a stable and happy family?

Some of the questions above may seem very trivial and many of us will just decide to take a view over time and see how things develop. Well done if that does work successfully for you. However, feeling resentful because we are being expected to shoulder more than our fair share of the nitty-gritty of family life or that our contribution (not in money terms) to caring for our family is not recognised by our partner will, like any resentment, inevitably spill over into other aspects of our relationship. It's much better to try to come to some agreement before things slide into an intractable problem.

4. How will we bring up our child(ren)?

Leaving out the effect our particular financial circumstances can have on how we bring up our children, in the main we tend to be influenced by four main factors – our religious views, our own childhood experiences, our cultural background, and our own personal philosophy of raising children. It is important to explore our own and our partner's views about how our children should be raised.

A: Do we expect our children to be brought up according to the tenets of a particular religion or political ideology?

If we and our partner have shared religious or political views then there should be little room for disagreement about how any children should be brought up. It is when there is a fundamental difference in views that there is scope for conflict, which, sadly, sometimes is irresolvable.

Case Study

Tania met Costas on holiday in Greece a few years ago. They were young and very much in love when they married within three months of meeting and Tania found that she was pregnant soon afterwards with their son, Simon. Tania felt blissfully happy until two years into the marriage when Costas came home to tell Tania that he had decided to join a small religious cult. Tania was very shocked as Costas had not told her that he was exploring any form of religion. Costas told her that from now on the celebration of birthdays, Mother's Day or Father's Day was forbidden and that they would only be socialising with other families within the community. Tania was very upset to hear Costas tell their son that there was no such thing as Father Christmas. Costas expects Tania and, therefore, Simon to join him in the community but although Tania has been with him to various meetings she feels that she could not fully participate in their beliefs. Costas has made it clear that he expects his son to be brought up in his faith and this has caused many arguments. Tania is considering leaving Costas but is afraid that he will try to take Simon away from her and deny contact if she is not a member of the community.

B: What were our own childhood experiences?
Will our experiences of our own upbringing influence how we bring up our own children?

Case Study

Tammi and Sim have three children. Tammi was brought up in a middle-class household where a lot of emphasis was placed on academic achievement. She and her two sisters played the piano and violin at an early age and each was expected to be top of the class in whatever they did. Tammi's parents put every single penny they earned into their children's private education but considered that a worthwhile investment. Tammi's mother always says, 'You cannot take an education away from anyone.' Tammi is keen that her children with Sim will be privately educated and that extra-curricular activities will centre on music, dance and cultural visits. Sim, on the other hand, is a successful property developer, having left school at 16. He sees no need to spend money on a private education for his girls, arguing that he did well out of a comprehensive education and that the money would be better spent on expensive family holidays and treats. He is not keen that the girls should be brought up in what he considers to be a 'hot-housing' academic environment, which will put undue stress on them. At the moment Tammi and Sim are unable to appreciate each other's point of view and are at constant loggerheads, which makes for an unhappy atmosphere in the home.

If Tammi and Sim had talked about their different views before the children were born then any arguments about schooling could have been had before the children were around to witness the tension between their parents.

C: What is our cultural upbringing?

Will our cultural upbringing influence how we bring up our child(ren)?

Every culture has ideas about how best to raise children to fit into the society into which they are born. If we are considering having a child with someone who has not been brought up in the same country or culture as us then discussing how we expect our children to be raised is even more vital. In Chapter Five we discussed the 'other family' where Kay, from Liverpool, was initially taken aback by Khow's strict attitude to parenting, which was rooted in his Chinese upbringing.

In international relationships it is worth discussing where we want our children to be raised, particularly if it is to be in a country with which we have little or no connection.

Case Study

Shelly met Eric when she was on holiday in the Gambia. Eric was a local waiter at her hotel and they had an intense holiday romance. After three years of a long-distance relationship Shelly and Eric married and after the birth of their daughter, Evie, Eric was granted indefinite leave to remain in the UK. However, he found that he could not settle in the UK, mainly because of the weather and because his employment prospects were very limited. Eric became insistent that they return to the Gambia as a family. He felt that Evie would benefit from a more traditional Gambian upbringing and education. Shelly was not opposed to moving to Gambia until she learnt that a high proportion of girls are subjected to female genital mutilation in Gambia.

When she questioned Eric he was evasive about whether Evie would be subjected to this practice. Shelly will not be moving to Gambia with Evie.

Although Shelly's experience is quite extreme, it can be a huge wrench to be expected by our partner to leave our family and friends behind. At least if we discuss the issue of where the children will be raised before they are born we can make an informed decision in the light of our partner's assurances (always bearing in mind that people can change their minds but that it is possibly more difficult to do so if the subject has been out in the open for some time).

D: Will our own personal philosophy influence how our child(ren) are raised by us?

Even in the enlightened days of the twenty-first century some people do have very set ideas about how children should be brought up. Do we or our partner have rigid ideas about how our child(ren) should be raised? Are we insistent that our boys will be great sportsmen or that it is not worth educating girls? Do we believe that children should go to boarding school at eight? Do we believe 'children should be seen and not heard' and that affectionate displays of love are not appropriate? Do we feel physical punishment is an appropriate way of disciplining our children or that little or no discipline is the best way to nurture our children? Do we feel breastfeeding children until they are five is healthy? Do we think that camping holidays in the rain are good for the soul? Are we insistent that our children will not eat meat?

Case Study

Monica and Sally have two children and on the whole agree on most of the big questions about how the children should be brought up. They are loving and carefree parents, spending a lot of quality time together as a family. The only thing they disagree about is Sally's insistence on the family only having access to television, computers or sweets and biscuits between 9 a.m. and 12 noon on a Saturday morning, when she and Monica do most of the household chores. 'It drives me insane,' says Monica. 'The children moan and are bored after they have done homework during the week. What harm can a bit of TV or computer time during the week do to them? I like having an occasional biscuit or sweet in the evenings but I can't because Sally says it would be hypocritical.' Monica has also noticed that the children gorge on sweet things when allowed to, rather than learning how to regulate themselves, and she suspects there will be terrible arguments later when the children become teenagers and it is much harder to police their access to technology.

We certainly do not want to put anyone off having children, whether you are able to conceive naturally or intend to adopt, use IVF, surrogacy or any other means, but we have attempted to flag up possible areas of contention and hope that honest responses to the questions we have posed above will lead to a more open discussion of what is expected by us of the whys and hows of having children. As with everything else, being realistic, honest and self-aware will enable us to make well-informed decisions about being a parent. Our children deserve, at the very least, that.

But what if we want and expect children to be part of our life together and it is just not possible? The shock and strain on a couple who are unable to conceive naturally cannot be minimised. Of course, there are medical interventions that can help and adoption, surrogacy and fostering are available to all couples (whether heterosexual or not), but we would say that in all cases it might be a good idea for a couple to access joint counselling before considering alternative means. All too often it is one of the individuals who is more strongly in favour of taking a medical route, adopting, fostering or surrogacy.

Case Study

Larry and Pauline had been trying for a baby for three years when Pauline insisted that they contact their GP who referred them to a fertility clinic. There they were told that IVF may be the only possibility of Pauline conceiving. Pauline was upset but adamant that she wanted to pursue IVF, although Larry was ambivalent. He felt they had a loving and close relationship and that children were not necessarily going to add to their lives. Larry felt that he had no choice but to go along with Pauline but became very resentful about the medicalisation of their sex life. Pauline was obsessed with having sex when she was at her most fertile and became moody and demanding when she began to inject herself with the fertility drugs. All in all Larry began to find Pauline's single-minded determination to get pregnant almost akin to a madness. Where once they'd had a fun and close relationship, Larry began to see it deteriorate into an overwhelmingly difficult one.

Pauline was devastated when three attempts at IVF

failed. She then decided that adoption was the next best option. Larry refused point blank to consider adoption as he felt their relationship was too fragile and strained to contemplate bringing a child into it. His refusal provoked a huge argument and Larry, at least temporarily, has moved out of their home. Larry feels that Pauline has put the fantasy of having a child way above and beyond the reality of their relationship and until Pauline can see Larry for himself again, rather than as a potential father, he has no intention of coming home.

***

It is not unheard of for some women (heterosexual or not) to use unsuspecting men as 'non-consensual sperm donors' with no intention of letting the father have close contact with the resulting child. In our experience this has never ended happily for the child or the man. A child has been wilfully denied a relationship with its father and the father has become embittered and frustrated in his attempts, through the courts or mediation/negotiation to have some sort of contact with their child. We would say this does not seem to be the act of a loving and caring mother and is storing up emotional trouble for the child.

Consider the following:

1. If it is not possible to have children together, would you be happy to consider IVF, sperm donation, surrogacy, adoption or fostering?

2. What would it mean to you and your partner to seek medical help to conceive a child?

3. What would it mean to you and your partner if a child was not genetically (or partially genetically) yours?

4. Could you and your partner accept that if it was not possible to have a child together, your relationship was sufficient?

Guidance

We cannot reiterate strongly enough that once we have a child with our partner we will be bound to them forever, whether or not the relationship survives.

Some of the saddest family law cases are those that involve bitter disputes between parents who are no longer in a relationship about the care of their children. Through no fault of their own some children become unwitting pawns in a complicated and, inevitably, destructive battle. When thinking of whether you want children with a particular partner please bear R.I.S.K. in mind. Be aware of the reality of having children, be honest, be self-aware and, above all, be informed.

Chapter Nine
Warning signs or possible deal-breakers

*'The mind in its own place, and in itself, can make a
heaven of Hell, a hell of Heaven.'*
—**John Milton**

And so can some people make a hell of what should be a
straightforward, loving relationship. When we fall in love
and plan a future together, as we said in Chapter One,
reality distorts for a while, but after around a year to a year-
and-a-half, clear-sightedness should return. We hope that
when we do float back to earth and reality we remain secure
and happy in our choice of partner but, unhappily, some of
us find that we have unwittingly become embroiled with
difficult, complicated or downright nasty specimens of the
human race and that our dream fantasy of 'happily ever
after' has turned into a nightmare of epic proportions.

'How did this happen to us?' we cry. But unless we have
been very unlucky and have fallen in love with a cunning
psychopath (who is able to coldly charm the birds from the
trees) there will usually have been hints of our partner's

true personality or intent towards us in the early days of the relationship but these, under the influence of the 'love drug', we will have ignored. Take this extremely sad letter written to Graham Norton in *The Saturday Telegraph* (21 March 2015):

Dear Graham,

Eight years ago, I met a man who swept me off my feet. It all sounds a bit fairy-tale-like but we seemed to fit together so well and I fell deeply in love. We made each other laugh, enjoyed the same pastimes, and nothing seemed difficult. The conversation between us flowed naturally and we were happy to spend quiet times together too. He had a career involving looking after the welfare of others; I felt safe with him, and I trusted him implicitly. Eighteen months after we met we had the most wonderful and romantic wedding and I quite simply couldn't have been happier. I honestly believed from the bottom of my heart that he felt the same way. A month to the day after we married he abused me physically. From nowhere his temper erupted and I ended up battered, bruised and completely bewildered.

So powerful were his protestations of love that in the early days I let these events go and put them down to the stress of his job. It wasn't long before he started to suggest that the reason for these outbursts was because he loved me so much; in his words, our love was powerful and dangerous, not to be messed with and I had hurt him in some spurious way causing these violent outbursts. I was so embroiled in this relationship that I couldn't see the wood for the trees, and it was only when I went to see a counsellor for severe anxiety that I realised in her words, there was 'an elephant in the room'.

Fast forward to now and I have finally left my husband: my decree nisi arrived on Valentine's Day (not the best Valentine's Day I have had!).

My question, please, Graham, is how will I ever get over the hurt that is with me every day from the minute I wake up? I'm not sitting around moping. I have a new job and am making new friends. But this feeling of heaviness in my heart seems to be there to stay and the tears come far too often.

The writer does not say whether she lived with her husband before the marriage (when there would have been less opportunity for her husband to hide his true temperament) and because she was so in love and caught up with the 'fairy-tale' of their relationship she chose initially to excuse and ignore all the warning signs that, despite the façade he had been able to maintain for eighteen months, her husband was in reality a dangerous and violent man. We hope that this unfortunate lady has been able to move on and put this terrible experience behind her.

Guidance
Some behaviour cannot be ignored.
There are certain negative behaviours that will inevitably overwhelm or cause major problems in long-term relationships, hints or warning signs of which should not be ignored or quickly forgiven, whether or not we are in the first throes of a committed relationship and whether or not many other aspects of the relationship are happy. On the whole, unacceptable behaviour will continue (no matter how contrite or sorry we are after each episode) unless and until the instigator is self-aware and sufficiently motivated to change or to seek professional help.

It is important to pay attention to any of the following behaviours and, please, do not overlook their significance, even at the beginning of a potentially long-term relationship:

a. Jealousy or unreasonable suspicion

A jealous nature can poison even the most promising of relationships as it stifles spontaneity and joy by causing unnecessary anxiety. Unwarranted jealousy and suspicion is usually rooted in insecurity but no matter how many times the jealous partner is reassured it will usually not be enough. As John Dryden said, 'Jealousy is the jaundice of the soul.' Constantly checking up on the whereabouts of a partner, checking their texts, email, social media or, at its most extreme, following or hiring someone to follow them is not a sign of love. It is possessive, controlling and downright destructive behaviour.

Case Study

Sally and Mark are both doctors in their late twenties and met at university. They are a good-looking couple, they work hard, like travelling and have lots of friends. All should be perfect and Mark knows that Sally does want them to marry and begin a family before they are much older. Mark is, however, greatly troubled by one aspect of their relationship: Sally's jealous and suspicious nature. Mark is a faithful and trustworthy partner but he has found Sally on many occasions checking his phone and emails for messages from other women (which she never finds).

'If we go out to a bar or for dinner Sally invariably accuses me of looking at other women and will cry and sulk when we get home. I find her behaviour childish and, frankly, insulting. I am exhausted tip-toeing around her. I am not prepared to spend the rest of my life worrying about whether Sally will throw a huge tantrum if I chat to a friend or patient who is female.'

****

b.   Unreasonable or extreme anger

There are some of us who have anger always just bubbling away under the surface ready to erupt at the slightest provocation, leaving our partner distressed and bewildered that such a trivial matter should trigger such an extreme reaction.

I had once seen a facet of his character that shocked me deeply. Angry over something I frankly no longer remember, he turned towards me with the face of an uncontrollable and malevolent child in a temper tantrum; his lower jaw thrust forward, his mouth contorted, his dark eyes narrowed. I felt this expression of out-and-out hatred went far beyond anything I could possibly have done to provoke it. I remember thinking, with total clarity, Who is that?
—Claire Bloom, *Leaving a Doll's House*

If we have been in a long-term relationship with someone who seems to have little control over their temper it's more than likely we will have seen countless incidents of unreasonable or extreme anger; we will know the flashpoints and we may have expended considerable energy in keeping everything calm to minimise the possibility of a meltdown. Over a long time it will become exhausting trying to anticipate possible situations that may trigger an over-reaction. In the early stages of a relationship there are probably two main situations that will trigger unreasonable anger and which if observed must be treated as warning signs of our partner's true underlying capacity for aggression: driving and eating out.

Case Study

Maurice and Toby met recently on an internet dating site. They are in their fifties, have both had previous long-term partners who have died, are financially comfortable and share a love of travel and fine dining. All seemed very promising at first but then Toby became aware of Maurice's propensity to fly into uncontrolled rages when he was driving.

'I'd noticed that Maurice always seemed very tense when he was driving but then I felt genuinely frightened when Maurice drove me out to Whitstable from London for a weekend getaway. We were held up in traffic getting out of London and I could see his face becoming more and more red – I thought he'd burst a blood vessel. He then drove at 90 m.p.h., weaving in and out of traffic and swearing at all other road users until I had to shout at him to slow down. When we got out of the car I was shaking but he did not seem to think there was anything wrong. I finished the relationship soon afterwards. I thought if he could be wound up so much by a bit of slow-moving traffic, what else would give him an excuse to kick off? I don't need that stress in my life,' said Toby.

Case Study

Casey met Theo at a bar in her local town. On their second date Theo asked Casey to dinner in a fairly smart restaurant. Casey laughs now as she recalls the date.

'I had dressed up and felt very special when Theo came to call for me at home in his car. He was very attentive, complimenting me on how I looked, opening the car door for me when we parked and generally making me feel like a princess. But the minute we were in the restaurant he behaved appallingly. He was rude to the waitress, telling her that she had not brought the menus to us quickly enough. He sent two bottles of wine back, saying they were corked, he complained that his steak was undercooked and that the vegetables were soggy. I was just mortified with embarrassment and kept smiling in a pathetic way at the staff. Theo kept saying that the staff had to be "kept on their toes". I kept thinking they were probably spitting into the food to get their own back.

'To cap it all, when the bill came he demanded that £20 be deducted because of the bad experience. As we left, our waitress came up to me and whispered, "Why are you with that guy?" As soon as we got back into the car Theo was charming but I could not wait to get home. I have ignored all his calls since then. I am certainly not getting involved with a Jekyll and Hyde character.'

Unpredictable and over-the-top anger in an adult can be very frightening, in particular to children. Do you want to subject any children to such behaviour on a long-term basis?

c. Unwarranted pessimism

Some of us are 'glass half-full' people and others, although not depressed, are most definitely 'glass half-empty', always ready to see the woe in any situation or uncover a conspiracy at the blink of an eye. On a long-term basis this attitude can be very draining and, as one friend put it, 'akin to being sucked dry by an emotional vampire'.

Case Study

Maria and Ted have been together for twenty years. Ted's habit of reading out to Maria gloomy stories from the daily national newspapers and concentrating on the bad news of their friends and community drives Maria mad. She has a difficult job as a social worker and is fully aware of the difficulties many people are presented with in their lives. 'I don't need Ted to remind me some people have it bad. What I do need is cheering up and being reminded that we have a good life, sufficient money, lovely children and a comfortable home. Ted is just so depressing I think it is beginning to make me depressed.'

d. Flirtatious behaviour

There's an old saying: 'Cast enough bread on the water and one little fish will bite!'

In other words, flirt or chat up enough people and no matter how dodgy you might be you'll probably get one person to respond! Some of us cannot resist putting the message out that we are available, whether or not we are already in a relationship. This can be seen as harmless flirtation that adds spice to a relationship but as time goes on it can be very wearisome to be with someone who just cannot resist signalling their availability to the world.

Case Study

Margie's father has always been an incorrigible flirt, something her mother seems to have chosen to ignore. Margie has always found her father's behaviour embarrassing and has been annoyed with her mother many times for overlooking his obvious flirtations (or worse). 'But even my mum lost her temper with him when she was struggling with a severe migraine at the supermarket checkout and found him trying to give his telephone number to the attractive checkout girl.'

e. Isolation tactics

This is a difficult one to spot because when we are in love with someone, at the beginning anyway, we want to spend all our time together, usually to the exclusion of family and friends. But beware of someone who subtly (or maybe not so subtly) begins to wean you away from your social group. They may profess a dislike for friends or family, they may demand that you spend every single waking moment with them or they may be so difficult and rude when you are with others that your group gracefully fades into the background. If you are in a new relationship it is vitally important that you maintain spending separate time with friends and family and do not allow yourself to become isolated, because it is much easier to be controlled by a partner within a relationship if you feel you have no one to talk to about any problems that may arise. If you are in a long-term relationship where you have become isolated from friends, family or community, please make a strong effort to reconnect. It is not healthy to become part of a mutually exclusive relationship, no matter how safe that makes us feel at the beginning of that relationship.

It is worth mentioning that under the Serious Crime Act 2015 the controlling or coercive behaviour of a domestic partner may be a criminal offence if that behaviour has a serious effect upon the victim. If a partner's controlling or coercive behaviour is causing you serious distress or alarm, please seek specialist legal advice.

Case Study

Jessie met Freddie through mutual friends. They are both in their thirties and both have children from previous relationships. Jessie was in a difficult relationship with Dan, the father of her daughter, Meg, and when she met Freddie she found him caring and very protective of them both. Very quickly, Freddie moved in with them and was very keen on cosy suppers and watching DVDs and TV, rather than seeing friends. This seemed delightful to Jessie, particularly as Dan had spent little time with her and Meg, preferring to be out with his mates until all hours. Slowly, Freddie started to be reluctant to see Jessie's family, making excuses when she wanted to take Meg to see them. Freddie then began to criticise Jessie's friends and if they did come around would be unfriendly and dismissive of them. Gradually, friends began to stop calling. But still Jessie does not see the warning signs as Freddie is always very loving to her and Meg.

A few days ago, Jessie's mother rang to ask her to go shopping with her and her sister and Jessie happily agreed. But when she put down the phone Freddie began to make a scene, shouting that if she loved him she would spend all her free time with him and no one else. He claimed her mother and sister did not like him and that they were trying to come between her and him and that they were using the shopping trip to 'poison her mind against him'. Jessie was shocked. She realises that she has hardly seen her mother and siblings over the six months she has been with Freddie and that her friends have begun to drift away, but although at some level Jessie recognises that subtly Freddie had begun to estrange her from her family and friends she cannot bring herself to finish the relationship. After all, Freddie loves her and Meg and, as he says, 'It's me and you against the world. Nothing else matters.'

f. The blame game

The 'blame game' allows either one in the couple to avoid taking responsibility for decisions made or things happening within the relationship. We often heard the words, 'If it wasn't for him/her I would have...' Fill in the gap: made lots of money; climbed Everest; got that promotion; been famous; written that book, etc. The fact that all of us have free will to do most things we wish seems very scary to lots of us and so it is much easier to blame someone else, particularly a long-term partner, for our perceived failures.

At its most extreme we see the 'blame game' being played out by people who have committed terrible acts against their partner and/or family. Like the mother who murders her children to stop the father seeing them and says, 'See what you made me do.' The 'blame game' usually starts with low-level criticism but can ratchet up fairly quickly in a relationship.

Case Study

Pete and Veronica have been married for twenty-five years and have two children now away from home. Veronica has always wanted to write a book but after two attempts in the early years of their marriage found she did not have the concentration or the imagination to be able to sustain the hard work or commitment needed to finish it. She has, however, convinced herself that she would have been a successful author if Pete had not insisted she return to work after the youngest was of school age, forgetting the fact that they'd had a big mortgage and that she had wanted the children to be educated at expensive private schools, which they couldn't afford on Pete's salary.

In any argument they have, Veronica returns to her theme of 'if it hadn't been for you I would have been a famous author', which Pete finds laughable. He says, 'If she had wanted it badly enough she would have fitted it in with work. Lots of writers manage it.' It's easier for Veronica to blame Pete rather than accept her dream of being a successful writer is based on fantasy, not reality.

g. Addictions

Any addictive behaviour of our partner but particularly concerning drugs, alcohol, gambling or sex/porn should set off a multitude of warning lights in a relationship. This is where a huge dose of reality and self-awareness is needed. There are those among us who love rescuing the damaged and there are those among us who are attracted to partners who seem a little bit on the edge; dangerous and exciting. But if we are in a relationship with an addict let us be very aware of the reality: the fact is that unless our partner is prepared to obtain professional help to conquer the addiction there will always be three in our relationship – us, our partner and the addiction.

And in many cases the addiction will always be our partner's first love. The reality is that it is usually very expensive to maintain addictions, so, unless money is no object, forget a financially stable future. The reality is that addictions usually render the addict self-obsessed and unpredictable so forget about having our own emotional needs (or those of our children) met and, if we have any shred of integrity, forget any moral qualms we may have about the drug/alcohol/gambling/sex industries.

Case Study

Susie met Harry at a dinner party. Harry was the life and soul of the party – loud, argumentative, very funny and obviously attracted to Susie. She was flattered by his attention and they quickly entered into a sexual relationship. When Susie was with Harry he made her feel 'alive'. There was a nervy excitement surrounding him that Susie found very beguiling but after a few months she found his unpredictability infuriating. Harry would make arrangements to meet and either turn up late or not at all, saying he was working late at the office. If he did turn up he would be anxious, distracted and sweaty, again excused by him by 'work problems'.

It was only when Susie mentioned to a mutual friend that she was seeing Harry that she found out the truth that Harry had a costly cocaine habit. When Susie confronted Harry about his drug habit he admitted he was in debt to his dealer but also said he had no intention of seeking help.

Harry said he could stop using cocaine at any time but felt he needed the help of it to give him the energy to cope with his demanding job. Susie was reluctant to give up on the relationship but as the months went by became even more disillusioned by Harry's unreliability and unpredictable behaviour. Things came to a head when Harry turned up at her flat with a black eye and injuries after his dealer had given him a warning beating about the mounting debts and Harry pleaded with Susie to lend him the money to pay the dealer off.

Susie broke off the relationship, although she was very upset. Susie genuinely thought that Harry would be motivated to curb his habit if he felt his relationship with her was under threat. Sadly, Susie was naïve and wrong.

h. Criminality

Some of us are attracted to the 'naughty boys and girls' of the relationship world. In the words of one woman, 'I like a man who's a player,' and by 'player' she means someone who flits around the edges of the criminal scene: a Del Boy for the twenty-first century. We make no judgement but only one observation: Naughty boys and girls care for no one but themselves so don't kid yourself that they will treat you in any way differently from how they treat the rest of humanity: as expendable prey.

i. Domestic abuse/violence

Research suggests that domestic abuse plays a part in one in four heterosexual and same-sex relationships, although in heterosexual relationships it is more than likely (but not at all necessarily) that the perpetrator of abuse will be male.

If we met someone and on that first meeting they publicly humiliated us, belittled us or hit us, then, unless we had masochistic tendencies, there is no way we would meet them again. So it is unlikely that in the first throes of meeting and falling in love with our partner we will suffer abuse or violence. It is more than likely that the abuse will start after we have formed an attachment or fallen in love with our partner, when it may be much more difficult to leave the relationship.

****

"The famous 'boiled frog' metaphor is a good way to demonstrate how domestic violence can happen so insidiously. If you dropped a frog into a pan of boiling water it would leap out immediately – and save itself. But if you put the same frog into a pan of cold water and the heated it up very slowly to boiling point it would first become soporific and lose consciousness – and only much later die. The gradual, infinitely small gradations of temperature increase (or intensity) are the key here. The creeping, surreptitious nature of domestic violence is what makes it so lethal."
—A Woman's guide to Divorce, Phyllida Wilson
& Maxine Pillinger

Domestic abuse is a method of controlling the relationship by fear. It is often conducted behind the doors of the family home and knows no cultural, class or social boundaries: a partner (male or female) in a high-earning, middle-class relationship can be just as likely to suffer domestic abuse as the stereotypical unemployed mother of four living in a high-rise council flat. Often partners do not want to report actual violence to the police because of the shame of outside intervention, or do not wish to separate from abusive partners because they want to keep the family together at all costs. The fact is, however, that it is rare for a perpetrator of domestic abuse/violence to carry out only one act and, indeed, when women do decide to report domestic violence it is generally accepted they will usually have suffered up to thirty-five previous incidents.

The problem of female violence against male partners seems to be increasing, although many men are reported to be unwilling to seek help or contact the police because of the stigma of being abused by a female partner. Support for men suffering domestic violence or abuse can be accessed through the ManKind helpline (www.new.mankind.org.uk) or the Men's Advice Line (www.mensadviceline.org.uk).

Since 2014 in the UK the Domestic Abuse Disclosure Scheme may allow you to obtain, from the police, details of a partner's past criminal history relating to abuse. It may be best to obtain legal advice about making an application from a specialist family solicitor or a dedicated organisation such as the National Centre for Domestic Violence (www.ncdv.org.uk) or a local Citizens Advice Bureau.

It is also worth mentioning that some research has shown that the biggest childhood contributor to male adult abusiveness is to be found in the relationship between father and sons: violent fathers are more likely to produce violent sons. If we allow our children to witness or suffer domestic abuse/violence in the home, how can they feel safe and happy or how can they form positive models of a happy family life?

Guidance
Whatever the excuse, if you are subjected to any actual violence by your partner then at the very least leave your immediate physical surroundings.

Do not keep silent about domestic abuse but tell close family and friends. Seek help from your GP or help from other appropriate agencies (check the Resources section at the back of this book). If you have suffered serious physical injury then co-operate with the police. Never minimise the significance of the first instance of domestic violence, either to yourself or your partner.

If you are subjected to a course of behaviour by your partner that is making you feel threatened, anxious, depressed or fearful, again speak up. Silence is not golden in these circumstances. By speaking out you may be saving yourself years of torment and indeed may prompt your partner to seek help.

And in particular please note the following huge flashing relationship warning sign:

Spitting is considered particularly relevant by various organisations (e.g. Relate) because it is generally the 'stepping stone' or linking action between non-violent and violent behaviour. It is a form of not-so-subtle conditioning or 'grooming' that habituates the victim over a period of time to expect (and accept) more and more extreme forms of abusive behaviour. If your partner has started to spit at you, it is time

to get out of the relationship fast. It is a sign of contempt.
—*A Woman's guide to Divorce*, Phyllida Wilson & Maxine Pillinger

There should be no excuses made for domestic violence or abuse. It is a gross breach of trust and anyone who tells us that they love us while abusing us has no place in our lives, no matter how emotionally or financially tied up with them we are, no matter how many children we may have with them or how long we have been together.

j. Emotional blackmail

Emotional blackmail is also a way of controlling the relationship by fear, although usually by the fear of what our partner will do to themselves or others rather than to us. Threatening to harm or kill themselves or spill relationship secrets to others can be effective ways of keeping a partner in a perpetual state of anxiety. If we do not comply with their wishes/threats and our partner hurts themselves (or others) they are apt to play the 'blame game'. 'Look what you made me do.' Do not under any circumstances give in to emotional blackmail or feel responsible for the actions of a partner who carries out any threats. Remember that we all have free will and we are each responsible for our own actions.

It may be a criminal offence if any attempt is made to emotionally blackmail us by making public intimate/explicit photos or videos we may have made with or for our partner. Do not hesitate to seek legal help or go to the police if such threats are made or carried out.

Guidance
As with domestic abuse above, if a partner is threatening to harm or kill themselves in an attempt to control you within the relationship, do not keep quiet. Tell friends and family or speak to your GP, or in extreme cases speak to the police.

k. Mental health issues
Becoming emotionally involved with anyone who has or has had serious mental health issues may require a huge amount of love, dedication and patience. Having mental health issues should not prevent a sufferer from having satisfying relationships but it is vital that we or our partner be completely honest with each other if we have mental health issues that could recur (such as clinical depression or obsessive compulsive disorder) or require continued medication (such as bipolar disorder) so that we can understand and support each other fully.

Guidance
If you become involved with someone with serious mental health issues, it is vital you obtain as much information as possible about your partner's illness and any medication they are taking.

Knowledge is key here. A good starting point is the website for the national UK charity MIND: www.mind.org. uk. This website sets out a huge amount of information and advice on a range of mental health topics, including how to help someone with mental health issues.

l. Personality disorders

The diagnosis of a personality disorder is fairly contentious even between mental health professionals, but there are two disorders that can cause havoc in a relationship: borderline personality disorder (BPD) and narcissistic personality disorder (NPD).

People with personality disorders often seem to have two personalities. Their problems aren't obvious until you have known them for several months or see them in a crisis. They appear normal or very exciting during courtship. They might be quite reasonable at work and with friends. But after you get really close to them for an extended period of time, they're no longer able to keep up this false self. They revert to their usual dysfunctional, extreme behaviour.

—*Splitting*, Bill Eddy and Randi Kreger

Guidance

So, we go back to our often-repeated advice: to discover our partner's true personality and attitudes, we must live with our partner for at least a year without making any major life decisions such as marrying, having a child or entwining our financial affairs.

***

People with BPD generally have a problem with perceived abandonment by their partner. Sudden and intense rages, out of proportion to any incident or dispute, are common, as is a recognisable pattern of a build-up of tension, rage and then remorse. At the beginning of a relationship with someone who has BPD we may have been swept off our feet and feel a heightened sense of unreality.

It is probably a lot easier to spot a partner with BPD than NPD as we will quickly witness their difficulty in controlling anger and rapid mood swings. People with NPD generally have a problem accepting criticism, being able to respond to a partner's emotional needs or at times separating fact from fiction. At the beginning of the relationship they can be utterly charming but very demanding. If they feel that they have been given insufficient attention or admiration a partner with NPD can quickly become verbally abusive while maintaining that they are the victim of a partner's inattention.

In the initial stages of a relationship beware the overly romantic gestures, the quick declarations of undying love, the fantastic bouquets of flowers, the expensive dinners, being swept off our feet by surprise trips away or any gesture that deprives us of a feeling of reality. Remember the letter written to Graham Norton that started this chapter: if it all feels like a fairy-tale, it probably is.

Guidance
If you have become heavily involved with a partner who you suspect has BPD or NPD, there are several books available (listed in Resources) that may help you understand the conditions.

It may be helpful for you to speak to a GP or counsellor. Under no circumstances should you tell a partner you suspect they have BPD or NPD before discussing your suspicions with a professional. It is usually the case that most people suffering from these disorders are extremely reluctant to access help.

m. Other behaviours

After dealing with the more disturbing warning signs above, we are loath to end this chapter with what can seem very trivial matters, but there are certain seemingly minor traits of our partner that can drive the relationship to the very brink if not addressed early on in the relationship. We have already flagged up time-keeping, untidiness and attention to hobbies in Chapter Three, but other honourable mentions must go to breaking wind, nose-picking, constant sniffing, swearing, grating laughter, knuckle-cracking, talking loudly or constantly cutting across a partner when they are speaking.

It may be that we don't mind any of those things in a partner but if we do and our partner will simply not listen to our concerns or, as often happens, bitterly resents being criticised, what does that say about our relationship? If any of these traits bother us then the earlier we address them the better, because the longer we go on the more irritating and annoying the habits will become!

Think about the following questions and see if there any warning signs flashing in your relationship.

1. Have you been swept off your feet by the intensity of your relationship?

2. Does the relationship have a fairy-tale feel to it?

3. Are you being pressurised by a partner to live together, marry/enter into a civil partnership within weeks/months of meeting?

4. Have you lived with your partner for over a year?

5. Does your partner check your emails, texts or social media?

6. Has your partner falsely accused you of having an affair or inappropriate relationships with others?

7. Is your partner unreasonably possessive or controlling in any way?

8. Does your partner tell you what to wear, read, eat?

9. Has your partner a quick-to-anger temper?

10. Do you worry about and try to prevent any situation that may trigger your partner's anger?

11. Is your partner prone to road rage?

12. Does your partner become unduly angry about service/food in restaurants?

13. Is your partner naturally overly pessimistic?

14. If you have been with your partner for any period of time do you feel emotionally drained because of their pessimism?

15. Does your partner constantly flirt with others in your presence?

16. Has your partner attempted to isolate or have they isolated you from friends, family or your community by being unnecessarily critical about them or hostile to them?

17. Does your partner blame you unfairly for things that have gone wrong in their life?

18. Does your partner avoid responsibility for decisions made in the relationship?

19. Is your partner an addict of any kind?

20. Will your partner accept treatment for their particular addiction?

21. Is your partner's addiction taking financial or emotional precedence over your relationship or towards your children?

22. Does your partner's criminal activities endanger you physically, mentally or financially?

23. Does your partner seek to control you by humiliation, verbal or physical abuse?

24. Have you sought to minimise any verbal or physical abuse suffered by you at the hands of your partner? Why?

25. Have you told anyone about any domestic abuse you may have suffered? If not, why not?

26. Does your partner seek to control you by emotional blackmail with threats to harm or kill themselves?

27. Has your partner threatened to emotionally blackmail you by making public any intimate matters between you?

28. Does your partner have existing mental health issues? Do you fully understand the nature of this mental health issue?

29. Does your partner have bouts of sudden and intense anger or rapid mood swings? Is this behaviour causing you distress or upset? Does your partner fulfil the criteria for borderline personality disorder?

30. Is your partner charming, exciting and persuasive but indifferent to your needs or those of others? Is this behaviour causing you distress or upset? Does your partner fulfil the criteria for narcissistic personality disorder?

31. Does your partner have annoying and irritating personal habits but will not listen to your concerns?

No one is perfect and during the course of a long relationship we are going to irritate each other from time to time, but the above relationship warning signs go above and beyond mere irritating habits. We can save ourselves a lot of future heartache if we are more aware of the signs of potential future bad behaviour and more aware of what we are prepared to tolerate in our partnership. We have to take the good and bad times in any relationship but when the bad times consistently outnumber the good then we have to reassess and ask ourselves one very basic question: why are we in this relationship?

We have the free will not to accept that we remain as victims (or martyrs) in relationships that are detrimental to our physical or emotional well-being. Seek professional help by talking to a specialist family lawyer or your GP or a counsellor, or access organisations offering specialist services through your local Citizens Advice Bureau.

Chapter Ten
Second (or third or fourth) time around...

'Marriage is a great institution.'
—**Elizabeth Taylor**

Even if we have found love again after a divorce, dissolution of a civil partnership or a final separation, unless we have been very lucky and 'consciously uncoupled' (read *Conscious Uncoupling* by Katherine Woodward Thomas), as Chris Martin and Gwyneth Paltrow announced a few years ago, it's very likely that although we may feel huge relief that we are out of a difficult relationship, we will still be carrying the heavy emotional baggage of shame, guilt and a sense of failure. In many cases we will also be presented daily with the physical representation of our previous relationship in the shape of our children.

We might have the same hope and expectations of love the second (or further) time around, but if we have not learnt from the mistakes that led to the failure of our previous relationship(s), what chance of long-term success will our new relationship have? And if we are bringing children from previous relationship(s) along with us, how do we know whether a new partner will have their best interests at heart or that our children will also grow to love him/her? The answer is that we don't – well, not at first.

If falling in love the first time and beginning a committed relationship is a huge leap of faith, starting all over again, possibly with reluctant children in tow, can be akin to setting off to climb Everest in trainers, in the fog and without a guide.

In our introduction to this book we said that when we were practising as divorce lawyers we were surprised time and time again by how many people jumped immediately into new relationships (or had overlapping relationships) even if their previous marriage or partnership had been horrendously difficult. Many of us seem to spend little or no time thinking about why our relationship went wrong before we commit to a new relationship, with most of us blithely assuming children, family and friends will immediately accept the new partner with open arms.

****

If you are contemplating beginning a new long-term relationship after the breakdown of a previous one then all the previous chapters in our book are relevant except that we feel the stakes should have been raised a little higher. If we have suffered the anguish of a permanent separation or divorce, particularly if we have children reliant on us emotionally and financially, shouldn't we be even more careful about who we let into our lives?

The more honest and self-aware we are, the better able we will be to make decisions grounded in reality. And the more realistic we are, the more likely we are to choose someone who is genuinely able to make us, and our children, happy on a long-term basis. We should be asking ourselves a number of questions before we become entangled with anyone else:

1. Were my expectations of my previous relationship realistic?

2. Was my previous partner capable of fulfilling my expectations of love, fidelity, emotional and/or financial support?

3. Was I honest in my dealings with my previous partner?

4. Did my own behaviour contribute to the breakdown of my previous relationship?

5. Am I too demanding, too difficult, too needy within a relationship?

6. Did I have affairs within the previous relationship?

7. Did my family and friends like/respect my previous partner? On reflection, were they right?

8. Did my previous partner like/respect my family and friends? If not, why not?

9. Did I tolerate my partner's infidelity, domestic abuse, anger or unreasonable behaviour? If so, why?

10. If my relationship broke down because of the infidelity, domestic abuse or unreasonable behaviour of my partner, have I been given adequate emotional/legal support?

11. Did I seek professional help for any emotional problems I may have had?

12. Did I seek professional help with my previous partner to address any relationship problems?

13. Am I attracted to potential partners with similar backgrounds, personalities or behaviours? Do such people make me happy on a long-term basis?

14. What have I learnt about myself from the breakdown of my previous relationship?

15. Are there things that I will now not tolerate in a future potential partner?

16. Am I seeking a new relationship simply out of fear of being alone?

17. Am I seeking a new relationship simply for financial considerations?

18. Do I have children from a previous relationship? What will be the effect on my children if I introduce a new partner into their lives?

If you have met someone who seems to be a potential long-term partner it is very sensible to ask them why their previous relationship(s) broke down. If they are unreasonably bitter, offensive or abusive about a previous partner, please take that as a huge relationship warning sign.

On the whole, problems in a new relationship after the breakdown of a previous long-term partnership should not be very different from those in any other relationship (and which we have flagged up in our previous chapters) except that certain problems can be exacerbated by children of previous relationships and money concerns.

1. Bringing children of previous relationships into a new relationship

If we have the primary care of our children from previous relationships, it is imperative that we be extra-vigilant in introducing a new partner into our family. Unlikely as it sounds, there are men who are adept at identifying vulnerable or lonely, single-parent mothers and inveigling themselves into the family with the sole intention of sexually abusing her children. It is not unknown for stepmothers to target wealthier men, diverting money to their own children at the expense of their partner's children, and open any newspaper on any given day and it is likely there will be a story covering a court case where a stepparent has physically or sexually abused their stepchild or even, in extreme cases, killed that child.

We are not saying that every potential stepparent is the wicked stepmother or stepfather from Grimms' fairy tales, that is obviously nonsense, but we are saying that if you are introducing a new potential long-term partner into your family, proceed with utmost caution.

Guidance

If you are beginning a new relationship and already have children from a previous relationship our one-year rule needs to be amended: don't live with any new partner for one year.

Have fun, try each other out but do not entangle yourself financially/emotionally for at least a year, and that particularly includes living with each other.

Children are often the bone of contention that plays a huge part in the decision to live in separate households. If the children are young and still at home, the tension of trying to meld two separate families into one is often more trouble than the partners find it to be worth; if the children are older and living on their own, and one or both partners has substantial money and property, the adult children often worry so much about inheritances that they throw up huge roadblocks when an elderly parent shows romantic interest in a new partner.

— *Calling it Quits: Late-Life Divorce and Starting Over,*
Deidre Blair

Case Study

Moira has two children with Geoff, Lucy, now aged twelve, and Tyler, aged nine. Geoff left Moira for her best friend and has gone to live in Spain with his new partner. He has had little contact with the children since he left the family home. Moira was extremely upset for around two years, during which time she and the children formed a very tight bond. In the past six months, four years since Geoff left, Moira has been seeing Sam, a work colleague, who is divorced and with no children. They get on very well and for the first time in years Moira is feeling happy rather than miserable. Last weekend she decided to introduce the children to Sam.

It did not go well. Lucy was sullen and rude towards Sam and his attempts to engage Tyler in a game of football in the garden ended in Tyler storming upstairs to his room in tears. Sam is pressing Moira to 'take their relationship to the next level' and for him to move in with her. Moira is torn between forcing the children to accept Sam and her relationship with him or Sam ending the relationship because he has made it plain that he is not prepared to continue just being an 'occasional boyfriend'.

This is a difficult situation and one that does not have an easy answer. Does Moira put her own feelings to the fore and allow Sam to move in now, disrupting their close family unit and upsetting the children when they are still at an impressionable age, or does she hold her ground with Sam, telling him they should continue with their separate residences, even though he may end the relationship if she does not agree to him moving in?

Our feeling is that just as what is in a child's best interests and welfare is at the heart of English legislation affecting children, so it should be that it is the children's best interests must come first in any decisions a parent makes. A truly caring and loving parent will not place their own emotional needs and wants above their children's best interests. This will not sit well with those among us who subscribe to the mantra that 'You only live once' (which seems to give us the freedom to forget our responsibilities and duties) but if we are to avoid our children being collateral damage in any relationship breakdown they should be at the forefront of our minds when deciding whether or not to embroil ourselves in a new relationship.

Moira should wait to get to know Sam over a longer period of time. The children need time to accept Sam, and if he is truly a decent man he will want to win them over slowly and not force the issue of moving into the family home. With her children's welfare at heart, Moira should be realistic and ask herself: why is Sam so anxious to push the relationship on so quickly? As they say in all the best detective novels, what is his motivation for wanting to move so quickly into her family home?

Case Study

Bruno and Fay have just married. They have had a whirlwind romance after they connected on an internet dating site. Bruno, forty-two, has been married and has three children under the age of fifteen. Fay, twenty-four has no children. Fay is a clever, caring and sweet-natured woman. She was aware that Bruno's children might be a little resentful of her and was determined to do all she could to win their approval.

'I never realised how hard it could be,' she says, after six months of out-and-out hostility from the children. 'The children are supposed to come to us every other weekend but often they refuse, which upsets Bruno a lot. When they do come they will hardly acknowledge me. The atmosphere in the house is tense and toxic. If I make a meal they are coldly polite but hardly touch it. Bruno veers from pleading with them to be nice to me to shouting and screaming. I hate it and end up crying for ages after they have left.'

And even if we have children who are adult and have their own families do not underestimate how hard it can be for them to see a widowed parent plunge headlong into new relationships. Some adult children find it very difficult indeed to see their parents as individuals with their own needs, wishes and desires outside a parental role but many feel a burning sense of indignation about a parent entering into a new relationship when the child feels a potential inheritance is at stake.

Case Study

Edna, a widow, and George, a widower, are both in their eighties. They met at their local church and have formed an intense and loving relationship. Edna endured a difficult and unhappy marriage for fifty years because, as she says, 'for my generation divorce was unthinkable'. Edna's son, Michael, who is in his fifties, is appalled and disgusted by his mother's new relationship. He has been very vocal about his disapproval to Edna and her family and friends and thinks her behaviour is tantamount to madness. In spite of Michael's disapproval Edna and George decided to marry.

At their reception Michael decided to speak, beginning his speech by looking at the aged guests and saying, 'Well, at least no one died during the ceremony.' Michael went on to bemoan the fact his mother was behaving badly and hinting that George was only after Edna's wealth, which George would ensure passed into his own son's hands. Needless to say, most guests left the wedding and reception with less than happy feelings. Edna, however, is blissfully happy and has no intention of letting Michael ruin her last chance of happiness.

***

But just as children can create problems about a new partner, it is not unknown for a new partner to bitterly resent children from a previous relationship and for the mother/father to choose a new partner over their children.

Although Philip's dislike of my daughter was transparent, as was his fierce competitiveness for my affections, I hadn't recognised how deep his prejudice ran where she was concerned. I was caught in the middle, with emotions and responsibilities tugging away on both sides; it was a no-win situation. Placing Philip's needs over Anna's meant hanging onto an important relationship at the price of my daughter's trust in her mother's protection; putting Anna's first meant keeping faith but surrendering a bond I felt with all my heart I couldn't live without. It was the choice between the security of a companion and the welfare of a daughter. Anna was asked to move out. She was eighteen.

—*Leaving a Doll's House*, Claire Bloom

We would have thought that any new partner asking a mother/father to choose between them or a child – unless in exceptional circumstances, say, where the child or children are of an age when they should be financially and emotionally independent of their parents – should be shown the door quickly and decisively. It's as simple as that.

2. Money the second time around

Moving on to a new long-term relationship after divorce or separation from a long-term partner, whether or not there are children involved, can have financial consequences over and above those already discussed in Chapter Seven. If we are receiving maintenance from a former spouse/ civil partner and we begin living with a new partner, our ex-spouse/ex-partner may well be entitled to stop those payments. If we are receiving benefits and begin to cohabit or marry/enter into a civil partnership then these benefits could be reviewed or stopped.

If we have already had to deal with difficult financial wrangles with our ex-partner, do we really want to automatically commingle any money/property we have in our sole name with that of a new partner? There is no room for hopeful, dewy-eyed naivety in this situation. We need to address the financial basis of any new partnership early on, particularly if we are the one bringing substantially more money into the relationship.

Case Study

Paul and Julie were married for thirty years when Julie announced that she wanted a divorce. Paul was devastated and was even more upset when he found that Julie was claiming a substantial capital sum as her interest in a family business, built up by Paul's family, in which Julie had never worked. After two acrimonious years Paul and Julie settled their financial claims and they are now divorced. Paul now has a new partner, Jane, who is living with him in a house purchased by him just after he and Julie were divorced. Jane is pushing Paul to put the house in their joint names as she feels 'insecure', and his refusal is causing arguments.

'I love Jane and I want the best for her,' Paul says. 'But I have no intention of losing any more money if this relationship breaks down. Jane has to take her chances with me that I'll do the right thing and look after her. She is in my will if anything happens to me and that's as far as I am going.'

Case Study

Mike and Joanna divorced amicably three years ago after being together for twenty-five years. They have two grown-up and independent children, Harry and Tom. Mike owns his flat and has a small machine-hire business, which produces a comfortable income. A few months ago he met Josie, someone he knew from schooldays. Josie is also divorced, is living in rented accommodation and is on benefits. The romance sparked very quickly and within a month Josie had given up her rented accommodation and moved in with Mike. Josie is now pushing Mike to marry in Las Vegas.

Harry and Tom are not happy about the speed of Mike's new relationship and have told him they think Josie is a 'gold-digger'. Mike is caught up with the excitement of being with Josie and has told his sons to 'butt out of my life'. He is looking at holiday brochures and seriously considering booking a wedding chapel. But Mike would be well advised to step back and reconsider. Once married to Josie, if the relationship does not last she will have potential claims on his property, capital and income. Mike is putting his close relationship with his sons under great strain and is risking jeopardising his current comfortable financial situation. He should be asking himself: why is Josie so keen to marry? Why is he prepared to be influenced by someone he has only really known for months over his adult children?

Guidance
If you are entering a new long-term relationship, have regard to the points we raised in Chapter Seven but also be prepared to discuss the financial basis of your new relationship very early on.

It sounds hard-headed but there is nothing wrong with asking your partner to show you bank statements, credit-card bills, and any other relevant financial information. If you suspect they have a dodgy financial history it is possible to search for records of county court judgments, etc. If you are seriously thinking about remarriage/civil partnership, seek legal advice about drawing up a prenuptial agreement. If you are considering cohabitation, consider a cohabitation contract.

What to consider on the second…or third…time around:

1. What do I know about my new partner's previous relationship history?

2. Is my new partner seeking to minimise any of their behaviour that may have caused difficulties in their previous relationships?

3. Has any former partner of my new partner caused trouble or arguments between me and my partner?

4. Does my new partner have any children from previous relationships?

5. Have I met my new partner's children?

6. How well do I get on with my new partner's children?

7. Are the children hostile towards me?

8. Will my new partner work with me to reduce any hostility the children may show towards me?

9. Do I expect my new partner to put my interests before any children?

10. Does my new partner expect me to put their interests (financially/emotionally) before any of my own children?

11. If there are recurring problems or arguments caused between me and my new partner because of any children either of us may have from previous relationships, are we prepared to consider family therapy together?

12. How does my new partner treat their obligations (financially or emotionally) from a previous relationship?

13. What do I know about my partner's financial situation?

14. Does my new partner expect me to alter existing financial arrangements in their favour?

When any deep and committed relationship ends, it is likely that our emotions will run high; we will feel angry, ashamed, guilty, sad, revengeful, betrayed, confused, anxious or maybe, just maybe, relieved. Our stress levels will be sometimes unmanageable and thoughts of the separation seems to dominate our very being, often making us behave in irrational and, frankly, at times bizarre ways. If our partner dies we can think well of them and remember their good points and the good times, but the sad truth is that with the break-up of a significant relationship we are more likely to have bitter memories.

If we are not careful our bitterness can infect our children, our family and friends until our former partner becomes a monster of mythic proportions. We would urge anyone who is tempted to turn children against their father/mother (no matter how badly behaved the ex-partner has been) to think again (and again). It is not unknown for an aggrieved parent to level allegations of abuse against the other to try to stop them from having any contact at all with their children. In our experience, all that happens is that the children will suffer badly for a very long time. It is understandable to have very destructive and negative feelings about an ex-partner who may have treated you very shabbily indeed, but a genuinely loving parent will never use children as a pawn in some kind of disturbed game-playing.

When our partnership has broken down it does mean that our dreams of the perfect relationship or family or lifestyle will have come to an abrupt end and a black hole of uncertainty has opened up in front of us, but there is no reason why another relationship cannot work – just as long as we learn from the breakdown of our previous partnership. Rolling straight into another potentially long-term relationship is not usually the answer, especially if our own habits, behaviours and expectations have contributed to the failure of our previous one.

And, finally, whether you have fallen in love for the first time or are embarking on a new relationship after the breakdown of a former partnership, beware falling into the trap of the 'stereotype relationship'. Are you one of the following types of couples?

1. The 'pipe and slippers' type

This couple are old-fashioned home birds. If they have children they may call each other Mummy and Daddy. If they don't have children they will have queasy nicknames for each other – anyone for Snuggle Bunny or Cuddlepops? TV and cups of tea are their chosen form of evening entertainment and weekends will be spent checking out car boot sales or visiting grandparents. There is an air of unreality about this relationship, with the troubles of the outside world kept well and truly at bay. This relationship will survive long-term as long as nothing or no one comes along to disturb its almost childlike innocence. This couple may pride themselves on never arguing, although from time to time at least one of them will make passive/aggressive comments about the other, usually leading to tears.

2. The 'on-the-up' type

This couple is ambitious and will be firmly agreed that they are going places. All is well with this couple as long as their career goals are attained, more money is made, more goodies are purchased and their dream lifestyle seems achievable. This couple will not survive long-term illness or unemployment in the relationship where the expectation that 'things can only get better' is dramatically interrupted or destroyed.

3. The 'Nelson approach' type

From time to time, turning a blind eye to our partner's foibles is probably a good thing in the long run but for some couples the 'Nelson approach' fundamentally underpins the relationship. Turning a blind eye to constant infidelity, criminality or dodgy dealing so as not to rock the relationship boat or maintain a particular lifestyle together will work so long as no one goes off with another partner or the law catches up with them. If this happens and the truth is forced out into the open, with no opportunity of ignoring what has really been going on, usually all hell breaks loose. These types of relationships often end in the most acrimonious of break-ups.

4. The 'look at us' type

This couple will maintain a glamorous exterior to the world. The clothes, the hair, the make-up, the look, holidays to see and be seen and flashy cars are all important to this type of couple. Youth or youthful looks are at a premium too and both will expect the other to be gym-toned and perfectly turned out in public. This couple is expensive to run and maintain and, unless lucky enough to be earning huge incomes, will usually fund the lifestyle with credit and/or debt. It is also tiring to be with someone who expects nothing less than perfection at all times, and woe betide a partner who is ill, puts on weight or begins to age. This couple can provoke huge anxiety in each other with the constant fear the other will go off with someone more attractive.

5. The 'unbalanced' type

Most couples need to be on a more or less equal footing as far as ambition, expectations and money are concerned for one or the other not to become dissatisfied. Certain individuals like relationships that lack that balance as it gives them more control in the relationship. They might be wealthier, better looking, more intelligent, better connected or more successful than their partner and will make sure, in an implied or implicit way, that their partner knows that they are very lucky to be in a relationship with them. Sadly, the more grateful we are for their attentions the more badly behaved they will become, with the ever-present threat that a more worthy partner may be just around the corner. Unless you are happy to be the ever-so-grateful supplicant, and possibly spend much of your time in distress, steer well clear of this type of relationship.

6. The 'I'm-only-with-you-until-someone-better-comes-along' type

Someone in this relationship will have made it clear, probably from the very beginning, that there is no long-term future in this relationship but that, for the moment anyway, while sex or money is on tap, they will grant us their presence.

This relationship (if it can be called a relationship) is rarely conducted away from the house (or bed) and we will never be introduced to family or friends. There is absolutely no point in indulging ourselves in wishful thinking that this relationship will magically transform into a long-term or committed partnership or that our loved one will suddenly realise the error of their ways and discover that we are the partner of their dreams. The reality is that relationships mired in contempt or that are conducted disrespectfully from the beginning are doomed. If we continually fall in love with people who treat us badly from the word go we need to be more self-aware and ask ourselves one question: why do I think so little of myself that I would allow another human being to treat me with such contempt?

If you are reading this book because a significant relationship has broken up, please, don't despair. There is absolutely no reason why after the breakdown of a long-term partnership you cannot find love and happiness again. Interestingly, on talking to past clients who'd had many years to reflect on whether, with the passage of time, they thought their divorce had been a good thing or not, none reported that they thought the divorce had been a mistake and many had gone on to form new long-term relationships that had given them great happiness. Trite as it may seem, in the long run wisdom, no matter how hard earned, can lead to greater contentment and happiness; it's just hell getting there!

Chapter Eleven
All's well that ends well

'It turned out to be the longest sustained period that Charbonneau and I had spent together, as a couple living under the same roof, and the time passed agreeably smoothly. The house and its setting helped – even in winter the place was beautiful – but the key factor in our mutual pleasure was that we enjoyed each other's company, which banal though it may seem, is the fundamental explanation of any successful and enduring union.'
—*Sweet Caress*, **William Boyd**

Why we fall in love with one person and not another is still open to debate. Is it down to chemical attraction? Do we unconsciously seek someone out who reminds us of a neglectful parent so that we can 're-parent' ourselves through our relationship? Is it all preordained so that we have no choice in whom we love? Whatever the reason, once we do fall in love, if we want that love to sustain us through many years, we cannot be complacent; whether by benign or wilful neglect, if we do not tend to our relationships they will 'wither on the bough'.

We don't have to be rocket scientists to realise that any mutual pleasure we may have in simply enjoying being in our loved one's company (or they with us) can quickly evaporate if we are treated badly by them by being held in contempt, constantly criticised, abused, treated unkindly or humiliated. Fear, loathing, or downright hatred of our partner has no place in a loving relationship, no matter how many years we have been together, how many family, social or community ties we may have, or how difficult it may be to disentangle ourselves financially.

In any dealings with anyone who comes in to our life, whether family, friends, work colleagues, foes and, particularly, our intimate partners, our constant mantra should be R.I.S.K: Realism, Integrity, Self-awareness, Knowledge.

****

Realism

If you are having problems in your relationship ask yourself: what is the reality of my situation? This involves taking a long, hard look at the situation you find yourself in. It might be helpful to write down your answers to the following questions:

1. When I am with my partner, for the majority of time do I feel, happy, loved and secure?

2. When I am with my partner, for the majority of the time do I feel anxious or unhappy or distressed?

3. When I am with my partner, for the majority of the time do I feel angry or bored or resentful?

4. Do I feel that my partner and I effectively and honestly communicate to each other any problems, concerns or issues in our relationship?

5. Does my partner listen to any concerns I may have and do they take those concerns seriously or do they usually seek to minimise my concerns?

6. How long have I known my partner?

7. Have I lived with my partner for over a year?

8. Do I feel that I have a rounded picture of my partner's habits, behaviour and personality?

9. Is there an air of unreality around my relationship with my partner?

10. Has my partner ever physically or verbally abused me?

11. Do I find myself making excuses about my partner's behaviour to myself or my family, friends or work colleagues?

12. What positive benefits has my partner brought into my life?

13. What positive benefits have I brought into my partner's life?

14. Has being with my partner adversely affected any area of my life – my relationship with my family, friends, community or my financial standing or my mental or physical health?

If, in answering any of the above questions, you have adopted a 'Yes…but' approach then stop and go back to the questions! Any attempt to excuse away the behaviour of your partner that is adversely affecting you shows that you are not facing the reality of your situation. Wishful thinking has no place in a realistic appraisal of your relationship. We can waste years hoping that our partner will change towards us by appreciating us or loving us in the way we expect.

Integrity

Being honest with others and ourselves should be simple, but often honesty can be too painful; how much better to blame someone else or our family or our community or the world at large for our problems? In intimate relationships it can be very easy indeed for us to shift the responsibility for anything that goes wrong onto the shoulders of our partner. 'Woulda-coulda-shoulda: if it hadn't been for you' is a common finger-pointing exercise in long-term relationships. It is very easy to mask our true selves to present a picture that we would rather show or be expected to show to the outside world but in a properly functioning relationship it is very difficult, if not impossible, for the majority of us to keep up the pretence without a partner noticing the disconnect between the truth and fabrication. Inevitably, the truth will out.

Ask yourself:

1. Am I being honest with myself about why I am in my relationship?

2. Is my relationship fulfilling the expectations or wishes of my family or community rather than myself?

3. Am I deceiving my partner about any fundamental issue in our relationship – money, children, sex, mental or physical health problems?

4. Am I able to take a 'third person' stance and acknowledge my part in any relationship problems?

5. Do I blame my partner for all or the majority of the problems in our relationship? Is this fair?

6. Deep down do I feel that I am being true to myself?

7. Deep down do I feel that I am being true to my partner?

Self-awareness

There is an old adage that says a person is made up of three things:

'What we think we are. What others think we are. And what we really are.'

And, although it might be difficult to be truly self-aware all the time, it doesn't mean we cannot have a go! If we can consciously think about how we have been treated in the past, our family upbringing, our family history, the community we were born into, our own basic temperament, our expectations, how we resolve conflict and how we present ourselves to the world and our partner, we feel that we will have a better chance of succeeding in our relationships. Being more self-aware gives us a better chance that we will be able to give of our very best to our partner, our family, our friends and the wider world.

If you are having problems within your relationship ask yourself:

1. Are my expectations of my relationship unrealistic?

2. Are my past experiences in my family upbringing/ previous relationships causing me to act to the detriment of my relationship?

3. Is it my personality or behaviour that is causing problems within my relationship?

4. How do I resolve conflict? Is my method of resolving conflict causing me to act to the detriment of my relationship?

5. Am I able to take a 'third person' stance and acknowledge my part in any relationship problems?
6. Am I prepared to seek professional help to become more self-aware?

Knowledge

'Knowledge is power. Information is liberating. Education is the premise of progress, in every society, in every family.'
—Kofi Annan

If we do not properly educate ourselves to enable us to make well-informed decisions within any relationship then we are trusting to luck and fate to ensure that we come through life without a care or problem. In the twenty-first century in the West we have unlimited access to a myriad of professionals, educational resources, the internet, the media (in all its forms) and numerous support groups and organisations designed to help anyone finding themselves in trouble. There is no need for anyone to be ill informed about any given issue that may be causing problems within a relationship. Read books (like this one!), seek legal or accountancy advice, trawl the internet and find out about support groups or talk to your GP before you make, or are pressurised into making, major life decisions.

Please remember to be cautious about sharing personal information with any individual/support group/organisation before checking their authenticity; this is particularly worth noting if you are accessing information via the internet.

***

Ask yourself:

1. Do I fully understand the financial aspects of my relationship?
2. Do I understand the emotional and/or financial impact of having children on me or my relationship?
3. Am I being asked my partner to agree to anything within the relationship (emotionally/financially/legally/sexually) the implications of which I do not fully understand or agree with?
4. Is my access to information being blocked by my partner?
5. How can I access information relevant to my situation? The internet, a library, books, a support group, a local or national organisation, a GP, a legal or accountancy professional?

Remember: Knowledge is power.

Life feels, for the majority of us, innately insecure but how we live our lives and with whom we live our lives can vastly increase or decrease that feeling of insecurity. We do not claim to offer a fool-proof system to guarantee a lifelong happy-ever-after state of bliss in your relationship but, in writing this book, we have tried to open your eyes to the common difficulties within relationships and get you to think about what might be applicable in your own life with your long-term partner.

We wish you the best of success in your life, both in your personal life and in your work, and we thank you for reading our book. We hope it helps.

Remember: Live a life of R.I.S.K: Realism, Integrity, Self-Awareness, Knowledge!

Bibliography

Albom, M., *The Five People You Meet In Heaven*, Sphere, 2004

Asher, R., *Shattered: Modern Motherhood and the Illusion of Equality*, Vintage, 2012

Blair, D., *Calling it Quits: Late-Life Divorce and Starting Over*, Random House, 2007

Bloom, C., *Leaving A Doll's House*, Virago, 2013

Bowlby, J., *A Secure Base*, Routledge Classics, 2005

Boyd, W., *Sweet Caress*, Bloomsbury Publishing, 2015

Byron, Professor T., *The Times*, 16 February 2015

Chapman, G., *The 5 Love Languages*, Moody Press, 2015

Cumming, A., *Not My Father's Son: A Family Memoir*, Canongate, 2014

Daily Telegraph and *Sunday Telegraph*, www.telegraph.co.uk

Daum, M., *The Unspeakable*, Farrar Straus Giroux, 2014

Dickens, C., *David Copperfield*, Penguin Classics. Revised Edition by Dickens, Charles, 2004

Eddy, B. and Kreger, R., *Splitting: Protecting Yourself While Divorcing Someone with Borderline or Narcissistic Personality Disorder*, Eggshells Press, 2011. Although this book covers the American Legal System it sets out good psychological advice.

Ephron, N., *Heartburn*, Virago. 2008

Evans, J., *Philosophy for Life. And Other Dangerous Situations*, Rider, 2013

Figes, K., *Couples: The Truth*, Virago, 2010

Financial Times., www.ft.com

Fuller, A., *Leaving Before The Rains Come*, Penguin, 2015

Gottman Institute., www.gottman.com

Grosz, S., *The Examined Life: How We Lose and Find Ourselves*, Vintage, 2014

Hawking, J., *Travelling to Infinity*, Alma Books, 2015

Hillier, J., Wood, H. and Bolton, W., *Sex, Mind and Emotion*, Karnac Books, 2005

Kabat-Zinn., J. *Where You Go, There You Are: Mindfulness Meditation For Everyday Life*, Piatkus. 2004

Larkin, P., *High Windows*, Faber & Faber, 1979

Lloyd, Professor E., *The Times*, 1 March 2016

Luard, E., *My Life as a Wife: Love, Liquor and What to Do About Other Women*, Bloomsbury Paperbacks, 2013

Macaro, A., and Baggini, J., *The Shrink and The Sage: Does Tidiness Matter?*, *Financial Times Magazine*, 27 September 2013

MacKenzie, J., *Psychopath free: Recovering from emotionally abusive relationships with narcissists, sociopaths and other toxic people*, Berkley, 2015

Marriage Foundation, www.marriagefoundation.org.uk

Mason, P. and Kreger, R., *Stop Walking on Eggshells: Taking Your Life Back When Someone You Care About Has Borderline Personality Disorder*, New Harbinger, 2002

McEwan, I., *On Chesil Beach*, Vintage, 2008

McGregor, Dr J. and McGregor, T., *The Empathy Trap: Understanding Antisocial Personalities*, Sheldon Press, 2013

Milton, J., *Paradise Lost*, Penguin Classics, 2003.

Mitford, N., *The Pursuit of Love*, Penguin, 2015

Moorhead, J., *Interview of Jane Hawking, The Guardian*, 16 May 2015

Nagoski, E., *Come as you are*, Scribe, 2015

Norton, G., *The Saturday Telegraph*, 21 March 2015

Office For National Statistics., www.ons.gov.uk

Pearlman, A., *Infidelity: A Love Story*, Broadway, 2001

Pregnant Then Screwed., www.pregnantthenscrewed.com

Rowe. D,. *My Dearest Enemy. My Dangerous Friend. (Making and Breaking Sibling Bonds.)*, Routledge, 2007

Sacks. O., *On The Move: A Life*, *Vintage*, 2016

Scott Berg, A., *Kate Remembered*, Simon & Schuster, 2013

Sedaris, D., *Dress Your Family in Corduroy & Denim*, Abacus, 2004

Searis, D., *When You Are Engulfed In Flames*. Abacus, 2007

Shakespeare. W., *The RSC Shakespeare. The Complete Works*, Penguin Macmillan, 2008.

Spiegelhalter, D., *Sex By Numbers: What Statistics Can Tell Us About Sexual Behaviour,* Profile Books, 2015

Strong. M., *Where on Earth are We Going?*, Texere Publishing, 2001

The Art of Couples Conversation., www.taoc.com.au

The Daily Beast., www.thedailybeast.com

The Guardian., www.theguardian.com

The Times and Sunday Times., www.thetimes.co.uk

Quotes from: Maya Angelou, James Goldsmith and Elizabeth Taylor., www.brainyquote.com

Quotes from: Leo Tolstoy, Edward Verrall Lucas and Malcolm X., www.goodreads.com

Von Arnim, Elizabeth. *Enchanted April*, Vintage Classics, 2015

Walsh, C., *Ask Me About My Divorce*, Seal, 2009

Wilson, P. and Pillinger, M., *A Woman's Guide to Divorce*, Robinson, 2015

Woodward Thomas, K., *Conscious Uncoupling: 5 Steps to Living Happily Even After,* Yellow Kite, 2015

Resources

Further Reading

Bancroft. L., *Why Does He Do That? Inside The Minds of Angry and Controlling Men.* Berkley, 2002

Cole. J., *After the Affair. How to Build Trust and Love again,* Vermilion. 2010.

Family Justice Council., *Sorting out Finances on Divorce,* www.judiciary.gov.uk 2016. This guide sets out in a straight forward manner how finances are sorted out on divorce/breakdown of a civil partnership in England and Wales.

Gerhardt. S., *Why Love Matters,* Routledge, 2015.

Johnson. Dr. S., *The Love Secret,* Piatkus, 2014.

Litvinoff. S., *The Relate Guide to Sex in Loving Relationships,* Vermilion, 2001.

Quilliam. S., *The Relate Guide to Staying Together.* From Crisis to Deeper Commitment, Vermilion, 2001.

Useful Organisations

Advicenow. This is an independent, not-for-profit website, run by the charity Law for Life: the Foundation for Public Legal Education. It provides accurate information on rights and the law including family and personal matters. It publishes advice leaflets including 'Make a Living Together Agreement' and 'Living together and breaking up.' www.advicenow.org.uk

British Association for Counselling & Psychotherapy. This association publishes a 'Find A Therapist' directory to help you find a therapist in your local area. www.bacp.co.uk

The British Psychological Society. This society offers various online resources to help you find a psychologist in your local area. www.bps.org.uk

Citizens Advice Bureau. This charity provides practical and legal advice about various matters including debt, housing and employment problems, and may be able to give advice on legal issues when problems occur in relationships. To find your local Citizens Advice Bureau: www.citizensadvice.org.uk

ICAEW. This organisation holds an online directory of 21,000 chartered accountants in the UK. www.icaew.com

MIND. MIND is a mental health charity and can provide invaluable information and support to anyone suffering from mental health issues or who is affected by someone suffering from a mental health issue. www.mind.org.uk

The Money Advice Service. This is a free and impartial money advice service set up by government, giving help about a variety of money-related matters including debt, budgeting, saving and investing, mortgages, making a will and dealing with finances on divorce and separation. 0800 138 7777   www.moneyadviceservice.org.uk

National Centre for Domestic Violence. The NCDV provides a free emergency injunction service to anyone who is a survivor of domestic violence. Phone: 0800 970 2070. www.ncdv.org.uk

National Domestic Violence Helpline. This is a national service for women experiencing domestic violence or their friends, family, colleagues and others calling on their behalf. 24-hour Freephone Helpline: 0808 2000 247. www. nationaldomesticviolencehelpline.org.uk

ManKind Helpline: This provides help for men suffering domestic abuse. www. new.mankind.org.uk

Men's Advice Line: This provides help for men suffering domestic abuse. www. mensadviceline.org.uk

Relate. Relate offers counselling services for every type of relationship nationwide (in the UK). They provide advice and counselling on every kind of relationship, sex, help with separation and divorce, and children and young people, and publish a variety of self-help literature. Phone: 0300 100 1234. www.relate.org.uk

Resolution. Resolution's members are family lawyers (in England and Wales) and other professionals who are committed to the constructive resolution of family disputes. You will be able to find a specialist family lawyer in England and Wales using the Resolution website: www.resolution.org.uk. If you are based in Scotland contact: The Family Law Association (www.familylawassociation.org) or in Northern Ireland via The Law Society of Northern Ireland (www.lawsoc-ni.org)

Samaritans. The Samaritans provide an around-the-clock, confidential service for anyone to talk about anything that may be worrying or distressing them. They are not a religious organisation. Phone: 116 123.

Tavistock Relationships (formerly known as: Tavistock Centre for Couple Relationships). This is an established London-based centre providing help with relationships, sexual problems, parenting and family life, and help with separation and divorce. TCCR offers counselling and psychosexual therapy on a sliding payment scale to ensure their services are accessible to everyone, no matter what your financial situation or how much you can pay. Phone: 020 7380 1975. www.tccr.org.uk

There are hundreds of internet forums, websites or groups on social media that are devoted to relationship problems or offer support. These may be useful for you to access BUT be very careful about sharing any personal information online and in the public domain unless you are absolutely certain of the authenticity and anonymity of the site. It's our view that you are better seeking professional support for any relationship advice or problems than relying on the kindness of well-meaning, but ultimately amateur, strangers.

Also available from Splendid Publications

**William and Kate's Britain -
An Insider's Guide to the haunts of the
Duke and Duchess of Cambridge**
By Claudia Joseph

Britain is an island with a rich cultural
heritage, which dates back to the Roman
era: it is a land of pubs and football; rock
music and opera; historic palaces and village
churches; breath-taking scenery and ancient
monuments. That's not to mention its
spectacular pageantry – the royal wedding
ceremony at St Paul's Cathedral and the
Queen's Diamond Jubilee celebrations were
beamed to billions around the world. Now,
in a unique guide to the British Isles, royal
author Claudia Joseph goes behind the scenes
– and reveals the secrets – of William and
Kate's Britain.

£9.99 (paperback)